# The Five Nations by Rudyard Kipling

Rudyard Kipling: A great Victorian, a great writer of Empire, a great man.

Rudyard Kipling was one of the most popular writers of prose and poetry in the late 19th and 20th Century and awarded the Noble Prize for Literature in 1907.

Born in Bombay on 30th December 1865, as was the custom in those days, he and his sister were sent back to England when he was 5. The ill-treatment and cruelty by the couple who they boarded with in Portsmouth, Kipling himself suggested, contributed to the onset of his literary life. This was further enhanced by his return to India at age 16 to work on a local paper, as not only did this result in him writing constantly but also made him explore issues of identity and national allegiance which pervade much of his work.

Whilst he is best remembered for his classic children's stories and his popular poem 'If...' he is also regarded as a major innovator in the art of the short story.

## Index of Contents

I0163432

"Before a Midnight Breaks in Storm"

Dedication from The Five Nations

Before a midnight breaks in storm,
   Or herded sea in wrath,
Ye know what wavering gusts inform
   The greater tempest's path?
    Till the loosed wind
    Drive all from mind,
Except Distress, which, so will prophets cry,
O'ercame them, houseless, from the unhintmg sky,

Ere rivers league against the land
   In piratry of flood,

Ye know what waters steal and stand
   Where seldom water stood.
      Yet who will note,
      Till fields afloat,
And washen carcass and the returning well,
Trumpet what these poor heralds strove to tell?

Ye know who use the Crystal Ball
   (To peer by stealth on Doom),
The Shade that, shaping first of all,
   Prepares an empty room.
      Then doth It pass
      Like breath from glass,
But, on the extorted vision bowed intent,
No man considers why It came or went.

Before the years reborn behold
   Themselves with stranger eye,
And the sport-making Gods of old, .
   Like Samson slaying, die,
      Many shall hear
      The all-pregnant sphere,
Bow to the birth and sweat, but—speech denied—
Sit dumb or—dealt in part—fall weak and wide.

Yet instant to fore-shadowed need
   The eternal balance swings;
That winged men the Fates may breed
   So soon as Fate hath wings.
      These shall possess
      Our littleness,
And in the imperial task (as worthy) lay
Up our lives' all to piece one giant Day.


## The Sea and the Hills

Who hath desired the Sea?—the sight of salt water unbounded—
The heave and the halt and the hurl and the crash of the comber wind-hounded?
The sleek-barrelled swell before storm, grey, foamless, enormous, and growing—
Stark calm on the lap of the Line or the crazy-eyed hurricane blowing—
His Sea in no showing the same—his Sea and the same 'neath each showing:
      His Sea as she slackens or thrills?
So and no otherwise—so and no otherwise—hillmen desire their Hills!

Who hath desired the Sea?—the immense and contemptuous surges?
The shudder, the stumble, the swerve, as the star-stabbing bowsprit emerges?

The orderly clouds of the Trades, the ridged, roaring sapphire thereunder—
Unheralded cliff-haunting flaws and the headsail's low-volleying thunder—
His Sea in no wonder the same—his Sea and the same through each wonder:
     His Sea as she rages or stills?
So and no otherwise—so and no otherwise—hillmen desire their Hills.

Who hath desired the Sea? Her menaces swift as her mercies?
The in-rolling walls of the fog and the silver-winged breeze that disperses?
The unstable mined berg going South and the calvings and groans that declare it
White water half-guessed overside and the moon breaking timely to bare it;
His Sea as his fathers have dared-his Sea as his children shall dare it:—
     His Sea as she serves him or kills?
So and no otherwise—so and no otherwise—hillmen desire their Hills.

Who hath desired the Sea? Her excellent loneliness rather
Than forecourts of kings, and tier outermost pits than the streets where men gather
Inland, among dust, under trees—inland where the slayer may slay him—
Inland, out of reach of her arms, and the bosom whereon he must lay him—
His Sea from the first that betrayed—at the last that shall never betray him:
     His Sea that his being fulfils?
So and no otherwise—so and no otherwise—hillmen desire their Hills.


## The Bell Buoy

They christened my brother of old—
  And a saintly name he bears—
They gave him his place to hold
  At the head of the belfry-stairs,
  Where the minster-towers stand
And the breeding kestrels cry.
  Would I change with my brother a league inland?
(Shoal! 'Ware shoal!) Not I!

In the flush of the hot June prime,
  O'er sleek flood-tides afire,
I hear him hurry the chime
  To the bidding of checked Desire;
  Till the sweated ringers tire
And the wild bob-majors die.
  Could I wait for my turn in the godly choir?
(Shoal! 'Ware shoal!) Not I!

When the smoking scud is blown—
  When the greasy wind-rack lowers—
Apart and at peace and alone,
  He counts the changeless hours.

He wars with darkling Powers
(I war with a darkling sea);
    Would he stoop to my work in the gusty mirk?
(Shoal! 'Ware shoal!) Not he!

There was never a priest to pray,
    There was never a hand to toll,
When they made me guard of the bay,
    And moored me over the shoal.
    I rock, I reel,, and I roll—
My four great hammers ply—
    Could I speak or be still at the Church's will?
(Shoal! 'Ware shoal!) Not I!

The landward marks have failed,
    The fog-bank glides unguessed,
The seaward lights are veiled,
    The spent deep feigns her rest:
    But my ear is laid to her breast,
I lift to the swell—I cry!
    Could I wait in sloth on the Church's oath?
(Shoal! 'Ware shoal!) Not I!

At the careless end of night
    I thrill to the nearing screw;
I turn in the clearing light
    And I call to the drowsy crew;
    And the mud boils foul and blue
As the blind bow backs away.
    Will they give me their thanks if they clear the banks?
(Shoal! 'Ware shoal!) Not they!

The beach-pools cake and skim,
    The bursting spray-heads freeze,
I gather on crown and rim
    The grey, grained ice of the seas,
    Where, sheathed from bitt to trees,
The plunging colliers lie.
    Would I barter my place for the Church's grace?
(Shoal! 'Ware shoal!) Not I!

Through the blur of the whirling snow,
    Or the black of the inky sleet,
The lanterns gather and grow,
    And I look for the homeward fleet.
    Rattle of block and sheet—
"Ready about—stand by!"
    Shall I ask them a fee ere they fetch the quay?

(Shoal! 'Ware shoal!) Not I!

I dip and I surge and I swing
   In the rip of the racing tide,
By the gates of doom I sing,
    On the horns of death I ride.
    A ship-length overside,
Between the course and the sand,
    Fretted and bound I bide
        Peril whereof I cry.
    Would I change with my brother a league inland?
(Shoal! 'Ware shoal!) Not I!


## Cruisers

As our mother the Frigate, bepainted and fine,
Made play for her bully the Ship of the Line;
So we, her bold daughters by iron and fire,
Accost and decoy to our masters' desire.

Now, pray you, consider what toils we endure,
Night-walking wet sea-lanes, a guard and a lure;
Since half of our trade is that same pretty sort
As mettlesome wenches do practise in port.

For this is our office: to spy and make room,
As hiding yet guiding the foe to their doom.
Surrounding, confounding, we bait and betray
And tempt them to battle the seas' width away.

The pot-bellied merchant foreboding no wrong
With headlight and sidelight he lieth along,
Till, lightless and lightfoot and lurking, leap we
To force him discover his business by sea.

And when we have wakened the lust of a foe,
To draw him by flight toward our bullies we go,
Till, 'ware of strange smoke stealing nearer, he flies
Or our bullies close in for to make him good prize.

So, when we have spied on the path of their host,
One flieth to carry that word to the coast;
And, lest by false doublings they turn and go free,
One lieth behind them to follow and see.

Anon we return, being gathered again,

Across the sad valleys all drabbled with rain—
Across the grey ridges all crisped and curled—
To join the long dance round the curve of the world.

The bitter salt spindrift, the sun-glare likewise,
The moontrack a-tremble, bewilders our eyes,
Where, linking and lifting, our sisters we hail
'Twixt wrench of cross-surges or plunge of head-gale.

As maidens awaiting the bride to come forth
Make play with light jestings and wit of no worth,
So, widdershins circling the bride-bed of death,
Each fleereth her neighbour and signeth and saith:—

"What see ye? Their signals, or levin afar?
"What hear ye? God's thunder, or guns of our war?
"What mark ye? Their smoke, or the cloud-rack outblown?
"What chase ye? Their lights, or the Daystar low down?"

So, times past all number deceived by false shows,
Deceiving we cumber the road of our foes,
For this is our virtue: to track and betray;
Preparing great battles a sea's width away.

Now peace is at end and our peoples take heart,
For the laws are clean gone that restrained our art;
Up and down the near headlands and against the far wind
We are loosed (O be swift!) to the work of our kind!


The Destroyers

The strength of twice three thousand horse
    That seeks the single goal;
The line that holds the rending course,
    The hate that swings the whole:
The stripped hulls, slinking through the gloom
    At gaze and gone again—
The Brides of Death that wait the groom—
    The Choosers of the Slain!

Offshore where sea and skyline blend
    In rain, the daylight dies;
The sullen, shouldering swells attend
    Night and our sacrifice.
Adown the stricken capes no flare—
    No mark on spit or bar—

Girdled and desperate we dare
　The blindfold game of war.

Nearer the up-flung beams that spell
　The council of our foes;
Clearer the barking guns that tell
　Their scattered flank to close.
Sheer to the trap they crowd their way
　From ports for this unbarred.
Quiet, and count our laden prey,
　The convoy and her guard!

On shoal with scarce a foot below,
　Where rock and islet throng,
Hidden and hushed we watch them throw
　Their anxious lights along.
Not here, not here your danger lies—
　(Stare hard, O hooded eyne!)
Save where the dazed rock-pigeons rise
　The lit cliffs give no sign.

Therefore—to break the rest ye seek,
　The Narrow Seas to clear—
Hark to the siren's whimpering shriek—
　The driven death is here!
Look to your van a league away—
　What midnight terror stays
The bulk that checks against the spray
　Her crackling tops ablaze?

Hit, and hard hit! The blow went home,
　The muffled, knocking stroke—
The steam that overruns the foam—
　The foam that thins to smoke—
The smoke that clokes the deep aboil—
　The deep that chokes her throes
Till, streaked with ash and sleeked with oil,
　The lukewarm whirlpools close!

A shadow down the sickened wave
　Long since her slayer fled:
But hear their chattering quick-fires rave
　Astern, abeam, ahead!
Panic that shells the drifting spar—
　Loud waste with none to check—
Mad fear that rakes a scornful star
　Or sweeps a consort's deck.

Now, while their silly smoke hangs thick,
    Now ere their wits they find,
Lay in and lance them to the quick—
    Our gallied whales are blind!
Good luck to those that see the end,
    Good-bye to those that drown—
For each his chance as chance shall send—
    And God for all! Shut down!

The strength of twice three thousand horse
    That serve the one command;
The hand that heaves the headlong force,
    The hate that backs the hand:
The doom-bolt in the darkness freed,
    The mine that splits the main;
The white-hot wake, the 'wildering speed—
    The Choosers of the Slain!


## White Horses

Where run your colts at pasture?
    There hide your mares to breed?
'Mid bergs about the Ice-cap
    Or wove Sargasso weed;
By chartless reef and channel,
    Or crafty coastwise bars,
But most the ocean-meadows
    All purple to the stars!

Who holds the rein upon you?
    The latest gale let free.
What meat is in your mangers?
    The glut of all the sea.
'Twixt tide and tide's returning
    Great store of newly dead—
The bones of those that faced us,
    And the hearts of those that fled.

Afar, off shore and single,
    Some stallion, rearing swift,
Neighs hungry for new fodder,
    And calls us to the drift:
Then down the cloven ridges—
    A million hooves unshod—
Break forth the mad White Horses
    To seek their meat from God!

Girth-deep in hissing water
   Our furious vanguard strains—
Through mist of mighty tramplings
   Roll up the fore-blown manes—
A hundred leagues to leeward,
   Ere yet the deep is stirred,
The groaning rollers carry
   The coming of the herd!

Whose hand may grip your nostrils—
   Your forelock who may hold?
E'en they that use the broads with us—
   The riders bred and bold,
That spy upon our matings,
   That rope us where we run—
They know the strong White Horses
   From father unto son.

We breathe about their cradles,
   We race their babes ashore,
We snuff against their thresholds,
   We nuzzle at their door;
By day with stamping squadrons,
   By night in whinnying droves,
Creep up the wise White Horses,
   To call them from their loves.

And come they for your calling?
   No wit of man may save.
They hear the loosed White Horses
   Above their fathers' grave;
And, kin of those we crippled,
   And, sons of those we slew,
Spur down the wild white riders
   To school the herds anew.

What service have ye laid them,
   Oh jealous steeds and strong?
Save we that throw their weaklings,
   Is none dare work them wrong;
While thick around the homestead
   Our snow-backed leaders graze—
A guard behind their plunder,
   And a veil before their ways.

With march and countermarchings—
   With weight of wheeling hosts—

Stray mob or bands embattled—
    We ring the chosen coasts:
And, careless of our clamour
    That bids the stranger fly,
At peace within our pickets
    The wild white riders lie.

Trust ye the curdled hollows—
    Trust ye the neighing wind—
Trust ye the moaning groundswell—
    Our herds are close behind!
To bray your foeman's armies—
    To chill and snap his sword—
Trust ye the wild White Horses,
    The Horses of the Lord!


The Second Voyage

We've sent our little Cupids all ashore—
    They were frightened, they were tired, they were cold:
Our sails of silk and purple go to store,
    And we've cut away our mast of beaten gold
                (Foul weather!)
Oh 'tis hemp and singing pine for to stand against the brine,
    But Love he is our master as of old!

The sea has shorn our galleries away,
    The salt has soiled our gilding past remede;
Our paint is flaked and blistered by the spray,
    Our sides are half a fathom furred in weed
                (Foul weather!)
And the Doves of Venus fled and the petrels came instead,
    But Love he was our master at our need!

'Was Youth would keep no vigil at the bow,
    'Was Pleasure at the helm too drunk to steer—
We've shipped three able quartermasters now.
    Men call them Custom, Reverence, and Fear
                (Foul weather!)
They are old and scarred and plain, but we'll run no risk again
    From any Port o' Paphos mutineer!

We seek no more the tempest for delight,
    We skirt no more the indraught and the shoal—
We ask no more of any day or night
    Than to come with least adventure to our goal

                    (Foul weather!)
What we find we needs must brook, but we do not go to look,
    Nor tempt the Lord our God that saved us whole.


Yet, caring so, not overmuch we care
    To brace and trim for every foolish blast,
If the squall be pleased to sweep us unaware,
    He may bellow off to leeward like the last
                    (Foul weather!)
We will blame it on the deep (for the watch must have their sleep),
    And Love can come and wake us when 'tis past.


Oh launch them down with music from the beach,
    Oh warp them out with garlands from the quays—
Most resolute—a damsel unto each—
    New prows that seek the old Hesperides!
                    (Foul weather!)
Though we know their voyage is vain, yet we see our path again
    In the saffroned bridesails scenting all the seas! (Foul weather!)




## The Dykes


We have no heart for the fishing, we have no hand for the oar—
All that our fathers taught us of old pleases us now no more;
All that our own hearts bid us believe we doubt where we do not deny—
There is no proof in the bread we eat or rest in the toil we ply.


Look you, our foreshore stretches far through sea-gate, dyke, and groin—
Made land all, that our fathers made, where the flats and the fairway join.
They forced the sea a sea-league back. They died, and their work stood fast.
We were born to peace in the lee of the dykes, but the time of our peace is past.


Far off, the full tide clambers and slips, mouthing and testing all,
Nipping the flanks of the water-gates, baying along the wall;
Turning the shingle, returning the shingle, changing the set of the sand . . .
We are too far from the beach, men say, to know how the outworks stand.


So we come down, uneasy, to look, uneasily pacing the beach.
These are the dykes our fathers made: we have never known a breach.
Time and again has the gale blown by and we were not afraid;
Now we come only to look at the dykes—at the dykes our fathers made.


O'er the marsh where the homesteads cower apart the harried sunlight flies,
Shifts and considers, wanes and recovers, scatters and sickens and dies—
An evil ember bedded in ash—a spark blown west by the wind . . .
We are surrendered to night and the sea—the gale and the tide behind!

At the bridge of the lower saltings the cattle gather and blare,
Roused by the feet of running men, dazed by the lantern glare.
Unbar and let them away for their lives—the levels drown as they stand,
Where the flood-wash forces the sluices aback and the ditches deliver inland.

Ninefold deep to the top of the dykes the galloping breakers stride,
And their overcarried spray is a sea—a sea on the landward side.
Coming, like stallions they paw with their hooves, going they snatch with their teeth,
Till the bents and the furze and the sand are dragged out, and the old-time hurdles beneath.

Bid men gather fuel for fire, the tar, the oil and the tow—
Flame we shall need, not smoke, in the dark if the riddled seabanks go.
Bid the ringers watch in the tower (who knows how the dawn shall prove?)
Each with his rope between his feet and the trembling bells above.

Now we can only wait till the day, wait and apportion our shame.
These are the dykes our fathers left, but we would not look to the same.
Time and again were we warned of the dykes, time and again we delayed:
Now, it may fall, we have slain our sons, as our fathers we have betrayed.

Walking along the wreck of the dykes, watching the work of the seas!
These were the dykes our fathers made to our great profit and ease.
But the peace is gone and the profit is gone, with the old sure days withdrawn . . .
That our own houses show as strange when we come back in the dawn!


The Song of Diego Valdez

The god of Fair Beginnings
    Hath prospered here my hand—
The cargoes of my lading,
    And the keels of my command.
For out of many ventures
    That sailed with hope as high,
My own have made the better trade,
    And Admiral am I.

To me my King's much honour,
    To me my people's love—
To me the pride of Princes
    And power all pride above;
To me the shouting cities,
    To me the mob's refrain:—
"Who knows not noble Valdez,
    Hath never heard of Spain."

But I remember comrades—
   Old playmates on new seas—
Whenas we traded orpiment
   Among the savages—
A thousand leagues to south'ard
   And thirty years removed—
They knew not noble Valdez,
   But me they knew and loved.

Then they that found good liquor,
   They drank it not alone,
And they that found fair plunder,
   They told us every one,
About our chosen islands
   Or secret shoals between,
When, weary from far voyage,
   We gathered to careen.

There burned our breaming-fagots
   All pale along the shore:
There rose our worn pavilions—
   A sail above an oar;
As flashed each yearning anchor
   Through mellow seas afire,
So swift our careless captains
   Rowed each to his desire.

Where lay our loosened harness?
   Where turned our naked feet?
Whose tavern 'mid the palm-trees?
   What quenchings of what heat?
Oh fountain in the desert!
   Oh cistern in the waste!
Oh bread we ate in secret!
   Oh cup we spilled in haste!

The youth new-taught of longing
   The widow curbed and wan,
The goodwife proud at season,
   And the maid aware of man—
All souls unslaked, consuming,
   Defrauded in delays,
Desire not more their quittance
   Than I those forfeit days!

I dreamed to wait my pleasure
   Unchanged my spring would bide:
Wherefore, to wait my pleasure,

I put my spring aside
Till, first in face of Fortune,
    And last in mazed disdain,
I made Diego Valdez
    High Admiral of Spain.

Then walked no wind 'neath Heaven
    Nor surge that did not aid—
I dared extreme occasion,
    Nor ever one betrayed.
They wrought a deeper treason—
    (Led seas that served my needs!)
They sold Diego Valdez
    To bondage of great deeds.

The tempest flung me seaward,
    And pinned and bade me hold
The course I might not alter—
    And men esteemed me bold!
The calms embayed my quarry,
    The fog-wreath sealed his eyes;
The dawn-wind brought my topsails—
    And men esteemed me wise!

Yet, 'spite my tyrant triumphs,
    Bewildered, dispossessed—
My dream held I before me—
    My vision of my rest;
But, crowned by Fleet and People,
    And bound by King and Pope
Stands here Diego Valdez
    To rob me of my hope.

No prayer of mine shall move him,
    No word of his set free
The Lord of Sixty Pennants
    And the Steward of the Sea.
His will can loose ten thousand
    To seek their loves again—
But not Diego Valdez,
    High Admiral of Spain.

There walks no wind 'neath Heaven
    Nor wave that shall restore
The old careening riot
    And the clamorous, crowded shore—
The fountain in the desert,
    The cistern in the waste,

The bread we ate in secret,
    The cup we spilled in haste.

Now call I to my Captains—
    For council fly the sign,
Now leap their zealous galleys,
    Twelve-oared, across the brine.
To me the straiter prison,
    To me the heavier chain—
To me Diego Valdez,
    High Admiral of Spain!


The Broken Men

For things we never mention,
    For Art misunderstood—
For excellent intention
    That did not turn to good;
From ancient tales' renewing,
    From clouds we would not clear—
Beyond the Law's pursuing
    We fled, and settled here.

We took no tearful leaving,
    We bade no long good-byes;
Men talked of crime and thieving,
    Men wrote of fraud and lies.
To save our injured feelings
    'Twas time and time to go—
Behind was dock and Dartmoor?
    Ahead lay Callao!

The widow and the orphan
    That pray for ten per cent,
They clapped their trailers on us
    To spy the road we went.
They watched the foreign sailings
    (They scan the shipping still),
And that's your Christian people
    Returning good for ill!

God bless the thoughtful islands
    Where never warrants come;
God bless the just Republics
    That give a man a home,
That ask no foolish questions,

But set him on his feet;
And save his wife and daughters
  From the workhouse and the street!

On church and square and market
  The noonday silence falls;
You'll hear the drowsy mutter
  Of the fountain in our halls.
Asleep amid the yuccas
  The city takes her ease—
Till twilight brings the land-wind
  To the clicking jalousies.

Day long the diamond weather,
  The high, unaltered blue—
The smell of goats and incense
  And the mule-bells tinkling through.
Day long the warder ocean
  That keeps us from our kin,
And once a month our levee
  When the English mail comes in.

You'll find us up and waiting
  To treat you at the bar;
You'll find us less exclusive
  Than the average English are.
We'll meet you with a carriage,
  Too glad to show you round,
But—we do not lunch on steamers,
  For they are English ground.

We sail o' nights to England
  And join our smiling Boards—
Our wives go in with Viscounts
  And our daughters dance with Lords,
But behind our princely doings,
  And behind each coup we make,
We feel there's Something Waiting,
  And—we meet It when we wake.

Ah God! One sniff of England—
  To greet our flesh and blood—
To hear the traffic slurring
  Once more through London mud!
Our towns of wasted honour—
  Our streets of lost delight!
How stands the old Lord Warden?
  Are Dover's cliff's still white?

## The Feet of the Young Men

Now the Four-way Lodge is opened, now the Hunting Winds are loose—
   Now the Smokes of Spring go up to clear the brain;
Now the Young Men's hearts are troubled for the whisper of the Trues,
   Now the Red Gods make their medicine again!
Who hath seen the beaver busied? Who hath watched the blacktail mating?
   Who hath lain alone to hear the wild-goose cry?
Who hath worked the chosen water where the ouananiche is waiting,
   Or the sea-trout's jumping-crazy for the fly?

He must go—go—go away from here!
   On the other side the world he's overdue.
'Send your road is clear before you when the old Springfret comes o'er you,
   And the Red Gods call for you!

So for one the wet sail arching through the rainbow round the bow,
   And for one the creak of snow-shoes on the crust;
And for one the lakeside lilies where the bull-moose waits the cow,
   And for one the mule-train coughing in the dust.
Who hath smelt wood-smoke at twilight? Who hath heard the birch-log burning?
   Who is quick to read the noises of the night?
Let him follow with the others, for the Young Men's feet are turning
   To the camps of proved desire and known delight!

Let him go—go—go away from here!
   On the other side the world he's overdue.
'Send your road is clear before you when the old Springfret comes o'er you,
   And the Red Gods call for you!


I

Do you know the blackened timber—do you know that racing stream
   With the raw, right-angled log jam at the end;
And the bar of sun-warmed shingle where a man may bask and dream
   To the click of shod canoe-poles round the bend?
It is there that we are going with our rods and reels and traces,
   To a silent, smoky Indian that we know—
To a couch of new-pulled hemlock, with the starlight on our faces,
   For the Red Gods call us out and we must go!

They must go—go—go away from here!
   On the other side the world he's overdue.
'Send your road is clear before you when the old Springfret comes o'er you,

And the Red Gods call for you!


## II

Do you know the shallow Baltic where the seas are steep and short,
    Where the bluff, lee-boarded fishing-luggers ride?
Do you know the joy of threshing leagues to leeward of your port
    On a coast you've lost the chart of overside?
It is there that I am going, with an extra hand to bale her—
    Just one able 'long-shore loafer that I know.
He can take his chance of drowning, while I sail and sail and sail her,
    For the Red Gods call me out and I must go!

He must go—go—go away from here!
    On the other side the world he's overdue.
'Send your road is clear before you when the old Springfret comes o'er you,
    And the Red Gods call for you!


## III

Do you know the pile-built village where the sago-dealers trade—
    Do you know the reek of fish and wet bamboo?
Do you know the steaming stillness of the orchid-scented glade
    When the blazoned, bird-winged butterflies flap through?
It is there that I am going with my camphor, net, and boxes,
    To a gentle, yellow pirate that I know—
To my little wailing lemurs, to my palms and flying-foxes,
    For the Red Gods call me out and I must go!

He must go—go—go away from here!
    On the other side the world he's overdue.
'Send your road is clear before you when the old Springfret comes o'er you,
    And the Red Gods call for you!


## IV

Do you know the world's white roof-tree—do you know that windy rift
    Where the bafing mountain-eddies chop and change?
Do you know the long day's patience, belly-down on frozen drift,
    While the head of heads is feeding out of range?
It is there that I am going, where the boulders and the snow lie,
    With a trusty, nimble tracker that I know.
I have sworn an oath, to keep it on the Horns of Ovis Poli,
    And the Red Gods call me out and I must go!

He must go—go—go away from here!
    On the other side the world he's overdue.
'Send your road is clear before you when the old Springfret comes o'er you,
    And the Red Gods call for you!

Now the Four-way Lodge is opened—now the Smokes of Council rise—
    Pleasant smokes, ere yet 'twixt trail and trail they choose—
Now the girths and ropes are tested: now they pack their last supplies:
    Now our Young Men go to dance before the Trues!
Who shall meet them at those altars—who shall light them to that shrine?
    Velvet-footed, who shall guide them to their goal?
Unto each the voice and vision: unto each his spoor and sign—
Lonely mountain in the Northland, misty sweat-bath 'neath the Line—
    And to each a man that knows his naked soul!
White or yellow, black or copper, he is waiting, as a lover,
    Smoke of funnel, dust of hooves, or beat of train—
Where the high grass hides the horseman or the glaring flats discover—
Where the steamer hails the landing, or the surf-boat brings the rover—
Where the rails run out in sand-drift . . . Quick! ah, heave the camp-kit over,
    For the Red Gods make their medicine again!

And we go—go—go away from here!
    On the other side the world we're overdue!
'Send the road is clear before you when the old Springfret comes o'er you,
    And the Red Gods call for you!


The Truce of the Bear

Yearly, with tent and rifle, our careless white men go
By the pass called Muttianee, to shoot in the vale below.
Yearly by Muttianee he follows our white men in—
Matun, the old blind beggar, bandaged from brow to chin.

Eyeless, noseless, and lipless—toothless, broken of speech,
Seeking a dole at the doorway he mumbles his tale to each;
Over and over the story, ending as he began:
"Make ye no truce with Adam-zad—the Bear that walks like a Man!

"There was a flint in my musket—pricked and primed was the pan,
When I went hunting Adam-zad—the Bear that stands like a Man.
I looked my last on the timber, I looked my last on the snow,
When I went hunting Adam-zad fifty summers ago!

"I knew his times and his seasons, as he knew mine, that fed
By night in the ripened maizefield and robbed my house of bread.
I knew his strength and cunning, as he knew mine, that crept

At dawn to the crowded goat-pens and plundered while I slept.

"Up from his stony playground—down from his well-digged lair—
Out on the naked ridges ran Adam-zad the Bear;
Groaning, grunting, and roaring, heavy with stolen meals,
Two long marches to northward, and I was at his heels!

"Two long marches to northward, at the fall of the second night,
I came on mine enemy Adam-zad all panting from his flight.
There was a charge in the musket—pricked and primed was the pan—
My finger crooked on the trigger—when he reared up like a man.

"Horrible, hairy, human, with paws like hands in prayer,
Making his supplication rose Adam-zad the Bear!
I looked at the swaying shoulders, at the paunch's swag and swing,
And my heart was touched with pity for the monstrous, pleading thing.

"Touched with pity and wonder, I did not fire then . . .
I have looked no more on women—I have walked no more with men.
Nearer he tottered and nearer, with paws like hands that pray
From brow to jaw that steel-shod paw, it ripped my face away!

"Sudden, silent, and savage, searing as flame the blow—
Faceless I fell before his feet, fifty summers ago.
I heard him grunt and chuckle—I heard him pass to his den.
He left me blind to the darkened years and the little mercy of men,

"Now ye go down in the morning with guns of the newer style,
That load (I have felt) in the middle and range (I have heard) a mile?
Luck to the white man's rifle, that shoots so fast and true,
But—pay, and I lift my bandage and show what the Bear can do!"

(Flesh like slag in the furnace, knobbed and withered and grey—
Matun, the old blind beggar, he gives good worth for his pay.)
"Rouse him at noon in the bushes, follow and press him hard—
Not for his ragings and roarings flinch ye from Adam-zad.

"But (pay, and I put back the bandage) this is the time to fear,
When he stands up like a tired man, tottering near and near;
When he stands up as pleading, in wavering, man-brute guise,
When he veils the hate and cunning of his little, swinish eyes;

"When he shows as seeking quarter, with paws like hands in prayer,
That is the time of peril—the time of the Truce of the Bear!"

Eyeless, noseless, and lipless, asking a dole at the door,
Matun, the old blind beggar, he tells it o'er and o'er;
Fumbling and feeling the rifles, warming his hands at the flame,

Hearing our careless white men talk of the morrow's game;

Over and over the story, ending as he began—
"There is no truce with Adam-zad, the Bear that looks like a Man!"

## The Old Men

This is our lot if we live so long and labour unto the end—
That we outlive the impatient years and the much too patient friend:
And because we know we have breath in our mouth and think we have thoughts in our head,
We shall assume that we are alive, whereas we are really dead.

We shall not acknowledge that old stars fade or brighter planets arise
(That the sere bush buds or the desert blooms or the ancient wellhead dries),
Or any new compass wherewith new men adventure 'neath new skies.

We shall lift up the ropes that constrained our youth, to bind on our children's hands;
We shall call to the water below the bridges to return and replenish our lands;
We shall harness horses (Death's own pale horses) and scholarly plough the sands.

We shall lie down in the eye of the sun for lack of a light on our way—
We shall rise up when the day is done and chirrup, "Behold, it is day!"
We shall abide till the battle is won ere we amble into the fray.

We shall peck out and discuss and dissect, and evert and extrude to our mind,
The flaccid tissues of long-dead issues offensive to God and mankind—
(Precisely like vultures over an ox that the Army has left behind).

We shall make walk preposterous ghosts of the glories we once created—
Immodestly smearing from muddled palettes amazing pigments mismated—
And our friends will weep when we ask them with boasts if our natural force be abated.

The Lamp of our Youth will be utterly out, but we shall subsist on the smell of it;
And whatever we do, we shall fold our hands and suck our gums and think well of it.
Yes, we shall be perfectly pleased with our work, and that is the Perfectest Hell of it!

This is our lot if we live so long and listen to those who love us—
That we are shunned by the people about and shamed by the Powers above us.
Wherefore be free of your harness betimes; but, being free, be assured.,
That he who hath not endured to the death, from his birth he hath never endured!

## The Explorer

"There's no sense in going further—it's the edge of cultivation,"

So they said, and I believed it—broke my land and sowed my crop—
  Built my barns and strung my fences in the little border station
    Tucked away below the foothills where the trails run out and stop.

Till a voice, as bad as Conscience, rang interminable change
  On one everlasting Whisper day and night repeated—so
"Something hidden. Go and find it. Go and look behin the Ranges—
  "Something lost behind the Ranges. Lost and waiting fc you. Go!"

So I went, worn out of patience; never told my nearest neighbours—
  Stole away with pack and ponies-left 'em drinking in the town;
And the faith that moveth mountains didn't seem to help my labours
  As I faced the sheer main-ranges, whipping up and leading down.

March by march I puzzled through 'em, turning flanks and dodging shoulders,
  Hurried on in hope of water, headed back for lack of grass;
Till I camped above the tree-line-drifted snow and naked boulders—
  Felt free air astir to windward—knew I'd stumbled on the Pass.

'Thought to name it for the finder: but that night the Norther found me—
  Froze and killed the plains-bred ponies; so I called the camp Despair
(It's the Railway Gap to-day, though). Then my Whisper waked to hound me:—
  "Something lost behind the Ranges. Over yonder! Go you there!"

Then I knew, the while I doubted—knew His Hand was certain o'er me.
  Still—it might be self-delusion—scores of better men had died—
I could reach the township living, but . . . He knows what terror tore me . . .
  But I didn't . . . but I didn't. I went down the other side,

Till the snow ran out in flowers, and the flowers turned to aloes,
  And the aloes sprung to thickets and a brimming stream ran by;
But the thickets dwined to thorn-scrub, and the water drained to shallows,
  And I dropped again on desert—blasted earth, and blasting sky . . . .

I remember lighting fires; I remember sitting by 'em;
  I remember seeing faces, hearing voices, through the smoke;
I remember they were fancy—for I threw a stone to try 'em.
  "Something lost behind the Ranges" was the only word they spoke.

I remember going crazy. I remember that I knew it
  When I heard myself hallooing to the funny folk I saw.
'Very full of dreams that desert, but my two legs took me through it . . .
  And I used to watch 'em moving with the toes all black and raw.

But at last the country altered—White Man's country past disputing
  Rolling grass and open timber, with a hint of hills behind—
There I found me food and water, and I lay a week recruiting.
  Got my strength and lost my nightmares. Then I entered on my find.

Thence I ran my first rough survey—chose my trees and blazed and ringed 'em—
   Week by week I pried and sampled—week by week my findings grew.
Saul he went to look for donkeys, and by God he found a kingdom!
   But by God, who sent His Whisper, I had struck the worth of two!

Up along the hostile mountains, where the hair-poised snowslide shivers—
   Down and through the big fat marshes that the virgin ore-bed stains,
Till I heard the mile-wide mutterings of unimagined rivers,
   And beyond the nameless timber saw illimitable plains!

'Plotted sites of future cities, traced the easy grades between 'em;
   Watched unharnessed rapids wasting fifty thousand head an hour;
Counted leagues of water-frontage through the axe-ripe woods that screen 'em—
   Saw the plant to feed a people—up and waiting for the power!

Well I know who'll take the credit—all the clever chaps that followed—
   Came, a dozen men together—never knew my desert-fears;
Tracked me by the camps I'd quitted, used the water-holes I'd hollowed.
   They'll go back and do the talking. They'll be called the Pioneers!

They will find my sites of townships—not the cities that I set there.
   They will rediscover rivers—not my rivers heard at night.
By my own old marks and bearings they will show me how to get there,
   By the lonely cairns I builded they will guide my feet aright.

Have I named one single river? Have I claimed one single acre?
   Have I kept one single nugget—(barring samples)? No, not I!
Because my price was paid me ten times over by my Maker.
   But you wouldn't understand it. You go up and occupy.

Ores you'll find there; wood and cattle; water-transit sure and steady
   (That should keep the railway rates down), coal and iron at your doors.
God took care to hide that country till He judged His people ready,
   Then He chose me for His Whisper, and I've found it, anti it's yours!

Yes, your "Never-never country"— yes, your "edge of cultivation "
   And "no sense in going further"— till I crossed the range to see.
God forgive me! No, I didn't. It's God's present to our nation.
   Anybody might have found it but—His Whisper came to Me!


The Wage-Slaves

Oh glorious are the guarded heights
   Where guardian souls abide—
Self-exiled from our gross delights—

Above, beyond. outside:
An ampler arc their spirit swings—
    Commands a juster view—
We have their word for all these things,
    No doubt their words are true.

Yet we, the bondslaves of our day,
    Whom dirt and danger press—
Co-heirs of insolence, delay,
    And leagued unfaithfulness—
Such is our need must seek indeed
    And, having found, engage
The men who merely do the work
    For which they draw the wage.

From forge and farm and mine and bench;
    Deck, altar, outpost lone—
Mill, school, battalion, counter, trench,
    Rail, senate, sheepfold, throne—
Creation's cry goes up on high
    From age to cheated age:
"Send us the men who do the work
    "For which they draw the wage!"

Words cannot help nor wit achieve,
    Nor e'en the all-gifted fool,
Too weak to enter, bide, or leave
    The lists he cannot rule.
Beneath the sun we count on none
    Our evil to assuage,
Except the men that do the work
    For which they draw the wage.

When through the Gates of Stress and Strain
    Comes forth the vast Event—
The simple, sheer, sufficing, sane
    Result of labour spent—
They that have wrought the end unthought
    Be neither saint nor sage,
But only men who did the work
    For which they drew the wage.

Wherefore to these the Fates shall bend
    (And all old idle things—)
Wherefore on these shall Power attend
    Beyond the grip of kings:
Each in his place, by right, not grace,
    Shall rule his heritage—

The men who simply do the work
  For which they draw the wage.

Not such as scorn the loitering street,
  Or waste to earn its praise,
Their noontide's unreturning heat
  About their morning ways;
But such as dower each mortgaged hour
  Alike with clean courage—
Even the men who do the work
  For which they draw the wage—
Men, like to Gods, that do the work
  For which they draw the wage—
Begin—continue—close that work
  For which they draw the wage!


## The Burial

**C. J. Rhodes, buried in the Matoppos, April 10, 1902**

When that great Kings return to clay,
  Or Emperors in their pride,
Grief of a day shall fill a day,
  Because its creature died.
But we—we reckon not with those
  Whom the mere Fates ordain,
This Power that wrought on us and goes
  Back to the Power again.

Dreamer devout, by vision led
  Beyond our guess or reach,
The travail of his spirit bred
  Cities in place of speech.
So huge the all-mastering thought that drove—
  So brief the term allowed—
Nations, not words, he linked to prove
  His faith before the crowd.

It is his will that he look forth
  Across the world he won—
The granite of the ancient North—
  Great spaces washed with sun.
There shall he patient take his seat
  (As when the Death he dared),
And there await a people's feet
  In the paths that he prepared.

There, till the vision he foresaw
   Splendid and whole arise,
And unimagined Empires draw
   To council 'neath his skies,
The immense and brooding Spirit still
   Shall quicken and control.
Living he was the land, and dead,
   His soul shall be her soul!


## General Joubert

**Died, South African War, March 27, 1900**

With those that bred, with those that loosed the strife,
   He had no part whose hands were clear of gain;
But subtle, strong, and stubborn, gave his life
   To a lost cause, and knew the gift was vain.

Later shall rise a people, sane and great,
   Forged in strong fires, by equal war made one;
Telling old battles over without hate—
   Not least his name shall pass from sire to son.

He may not meet the onsweep of our van
   In the doomed city when we close the score;
Yet o'er his grave—his grave that holds a man—
   Our deep-tongued guns shall answer his once more!


## The Palace

When I was King and a Mason—a Master proven and skilled—
I cleared me ground for a Palace such as a King should build.
I decreed and dug down to my levels. Presently, under the silt,
I came on the wreck of a Palace such as a King had built.

There was no worth in the fashion—there was no wit in the plan—
Hither and thither, aimless, the ruined footings ran—
Masonry, brute, mishandled, but careen on every stone:
"After me cometh a Builder. Tell him, I too have known."

Swift to my use in my trenches, where my well-planned ground-works grew,
I tumbled his quoins and his ashlars, and cut and reset them anew.
Lime I milled of his marbles; burned it, slacked it, and spread;

Taking and leaving at pleasure the gifts of the humble dead.

Yet I despised not nor gloried; yet, as we wrenched them apart,
I read in the razed foundations the heart of that builder's heart.
As he had risen and pleaded, so did I understand
The form of the dream he had followed in the face of the thing he had planned.

When I was a King and a Mason—in the open noon of my pride,
They sent me a Word from the Darkness—They whispered and called me aside.
They said—"The end is forbidden." They said—"Thy use is fulfilled.
"Thy Palace shall stand as that other's—the spoil of a King who shall build."

I called my men from my trenches, my quarries, my wharves, and my sheers.
All I had wrought I abandoned to the faith of the faithless years.
Only I cut on the timber—only I carved on the stone:
"After me cometh a Builder. Tell him, I too have known!"

## Sussex

God gave all men all earth to love,
    But since our hearts are small,
Ordained for each one spot should prove
    Belovèd over all;
That, as He watched Creation's birth,
    So we, in godlike mood,
May of our love create our earth
    And see that it is good.

So one shall Baltic pines content,
    As one some Surrey glade,
Or one the palm-grove's droned lament
    Before Levuka's Trade.
Each to his choice, and I rejoice
    The lot has fallen to me
In a fair ground—in a fair ground—
    Yea, Sussex by the sea!

No tender-hearted garden crowns,
    No bosomed woods adorn
Our blunt, bow-headed, whale-backed Downs,
    But gnarled and writhen thorn—
Bare slopes where chasing shadows skim,
    And, through the gaps revealed,
Belt upon belt, the wooded, dim,
    Blue goodness of the Weald.

Clean of officious fence or hedge,
    Half-wild and wholly tame,
The wise turf cloaks the white cliff edge
    As when the Romans came.
What sign of those that fought and died
    At shift of sword and sword?
The barrow and the camp abide,
    The sunlight and the sward.

Here leaps ashore the full Sou'west
    All heavy-winged with brine,
Here lies above the folded crest
    The Channel's leaden line;
And here the sea-fogs lap and cling,
    And here, each warning each,
The sheep-bells and the ship-bells ring
    Along the hidden beach.

We have no waters to delight
    Our broad and brookless vales—
Only the dewpond on the height
    Unfed, that never fails—
Whereby no tattered herbage tells
    Which way the season flies—
Only our close-bit thyme that smells
    Like dawn in Paradise.

Here through the strong and shadeless days
    The tinkling silence thrills;
Or little, lost, Down churches praise
    The Lord who made the hills:
But here the Old Gods guard their round,
    And, in her secret heart,
The heathen kingdom Wilfrid found
    Dreams, as she dwells, apart.

Though all the rest were all my share,
    With equal soul I'd see
Her nine-and-thirty sisters fair,
    Yet none more fair than she.
Choose ye your need from Thames to Tweed,
    And I will choose instead
Such lands as lie 'twixt Rake and Rye,
    Black Down and Beachy Head.

I will go out against the sun
    Where the rolled scarp retires,
And the Long Man of Wilmington

Looks naked toward the shires;
And east till doubling Rother crawls
  To find the fickle tide,
By dry and sea-forgotten walls,
  Our ports of stranded pride.

I will go north about the shaws
  And the deep ghylls that breed
Huge oaks and old, the which we hold
  No more than Sussex weed;
Or south where windy Piddinghoe's
  Begilded dolphin veers
And red beside wide-bankèd Ouse
  Lie down our Sussex steers.

So to the land our hearts we give
  Till the sure magic strike,
And Memory, Use, and Love make live
  Us and our fields alike—
That deeper than our speech and thought,
  Beyond our reason's sway,
Clay of the pit whence we were wrought
  Yearns to its fellow-clay.

God gives all men all earth to love,
  But since man's heart is small,
Ordains for each one spot shall prove
  Beloved over all.
Each to his choice, and I rejoice
  The lot has fallen to me
In a fair ground—in a fair ground—
  Yea, Sussex by the sea!

## Song of the Wise Children

When the darkened Fifties dip to the North,
  And frost and the fog divide the air,
And the day is dead at his breaking-forth,
  Sirs, it is bitter beneath the Bear!

Far to Southward they wheel and glance,
  The million molten spears of morn—
The spears of our deliverance
  That shine on the house where we were born.

Flying-fish about our bows,

Flying sea-fires in our wake:
This is the road to our Father's House,
    Whither we go for our souls' sake!

We have forfeited our birthright,
    We have forsaken. all things meet;
We have forgotten the look of light,
    We have forgotten the scent of heat.

They that walk with shaded brows,
    Year by year in a shining land,
They be men of our Father's House,
    They shall receive us and understand.

We shall go back by the boltless doors,
    To the life unaltered our childhood knew—
To the naked feet on the cool, dark floors,
    And the high-celled rooms that the Trade blows through:

To the trumpet-flowers and the moon beyond,
    And the tree-toad's chorus drowning all—
And the lisp of the split banana-frond
    That talked us to sleep when we were small.

The wayside magic, the threshold spells,
    Shall soon undo what the North has done—
Because of the sights and the sounds and the smells
    That ran with our youth in the eye of the sun.

And Earth accepting shall ask no vows,
    Nor the Sea our love, nor our lover the Sky.
When we return to our Father's House
    Only the English shall wonder why!


## Buddha at Kamakura

**"And there is a Japanese idol at Kamakura"**

O ye who tread the Narrow Way
By Tophet-flare to judgment Day,
Be gentle when "the heathen" pray
    To Buddha at Kamakura!

To him the Way, the Law, apart,
Whom Maya held beneath her heart,
Ananda's Lord, the Bodhisat,

The Buddha of Kamakura.

For though he neither burns nor sees,
Nor hears ye thank your Deities,
Ye have not sinned with such as these,
    His children at Kamakura,

Yet spare us still the Western joke
When joss-sticks turn to scented smoke
The little sins of little folk
    That worship at Kamakura—

The grey-robed, gay-sashed butterflies
That flit beneath the Master's eyes.
He is beyond the Mysteries
    But loves them at Kamakura.

And whoso will, from Pride released,
Contemning neither creed nor priest,
May feel the Soul of all the East
    About him at Kamakura.

Yea, every tale Ananda heard,
Of birth as fish or beast or bird,
While yet in lives the Master stirred,
    The warm wind brings Kamakura.

Till drowsy eyelids seem to see
A-flower 'neath her golden htee
The Shwe-Dagon flare easterly
    From Burmah to Kamakura,

And down the loaded air there comes
The thunder of Thibetan drums,
And droned—"Om mane padme hums"—
    A world's-width from Kamakura.

Yet Brahmans rule Benares still,
Buddh-Gaya's ruins pit the hill,
And beef-fed zealots threaten ill
    To Buddha and Kamakura.

A tourist-show, a legend told,
A rusting bulk of bronze and gold,
So much, and scarce so much, ye hold
    The meaning of Kamakura?

But when the morning prayer is prayed,

Think, ere ye pass to strife and trade,
Is God in human image made
    No nearer than Kamakura?


The White Man's Burden

**The United States and the Philippine Islands**

Take up the White Man's burden—
Send forth the best ye breed—
Go bind your sons to exile
To serve your captives' need;
To wait in heavy harness,
On fluttered folk and wild—
Your new-caught, sullen peoples,
Half-devil and half-child.

Take up the White Man's Burden—
In patience to abide,
To veil the threat of terror
And check the show of pride;
By open speech and simple,
An hundred times made plain,
To seek another's profit,
And work another's gain.

Take up the White Man's burden—
The savage wars of peace—
Fill full the mouth of Famine
And bid the sickness cease;
And when your goal is nearest
The end for others sought,
Watch Sloth and heathen Folly
Bring all your hope to nought.

Take up the White Man's burden—
No tawdry rule of kings,
But toil of serf and sweeper—
The tale of common things.
The ports ye shall not enter,
The roads ye shall not tread,
Go make them with your living,
And mark them with your dead.

Take up the White Man's burden—
And reap his old reward:

The blame of those ye better,
The hate of those ye guard—
The cry of hosts ye humour
(Ah, slowly!) toward the light:—
"Why brought ye us from bondage,
"Our loved Egyptian night?"

Take up the White Man's burden—
Ye dare not stoop to less—
Nor call too loud on Freedom
To cloak your weariness;
By all ye cry or whisper,
By all ye leave or do,
The silent, sullen peoples
Shall weigh your Gods and you.

Take up the White Man's burden—
Have done with childish days—
The lightly proffered laurel,
The easy, ungrudged praise.
Comes now, to search your manhood
Through all the thankless years,
Cold, edged with dear-bought wisdom,
The judgment of your peers!


## Pharaoh and the Sergeant

*" . . . Consider that the meritorious services of the Sergeant Instructors attached to the Egyptian Army have been inadequately acknowledged . . . To the excellence of their work is mainly due the great improvement that has taken place in the soldiers of H.H. the Khedive."*
*— EXTRACT FROM LETTER.*

Said England unto Pharaoh, "I must make a man of you,
    That will stand upon his feet and play the game;
That will Maxim his oppressor as a Christian ought to do,"
    And she sent old Pharaoh Sergeant Whatisname.
        It was not a Duke nor Earl, nor yet a Viscount—
            It was not a big brass General that came;
        But a man in khaki kit who could handle men a bit,
            With his bedding labelled Sergeant Whatisname.

Said England unto Pharaoh, "Though at present singing small,
    You shall hum a proper tune before it ends,"
And she introduced old Pharaoh to the Sergeant once for all,
    And left 'em in the desert making friends,
        It was not a Crystal Palace nor Cathedral;

It was not a public-house of common fame;
  But a piece of red-hot sand, with a palm on either hand,
    And a little hut for Sergeant Whatisname.

Said England unto Pharaoh, "You've had miracles before,
  When Aaron struck your rivers into blood;
But if you watch the Sergeant he can show you something more.
  He's a charm for making riflemen from mud."
    It was neither Hindustani, French, nor Coptics;
      It was odds and ends and leavings of the same,
    Translated by a stick (which is really half the trick),
      And Pharaoh harked to Sergeant Whatisname.

(There were years that no one talked of; there were times of horrid doubt—
  There was faith and hope and whacking and despair—
While the Sergeant gave the Cautions and he combed old Pharaoh out,
  And England didn't seem to know nor care.
    That is England's awful way o' doing business—
      She would serve her God (or Gordon) just the same—
    For she thinks her Empire still is the Strand and Holborn Hill,
      And she didn't think of Sergeant Whatisname.)

Said England to the Sergeant, "You can let my people go!"
  (England used 'em cheap and nasty from the start),
And they entered 'em in battle on a most astonished foe—
  But the Sergeant he had hardened Pharaoh's heart
    Which was broke, along of all the plagues of Egypt,
      Three thousand years before the Sergeant came—
    And he mended it again in a little more than ten,
      Till Pharaoh fought like Sergeant Whatisname.

It was wicked bad campaigning (cheap and nasty from the first),
  There was heat and dust and coolie-work and sun,
There were vipers, flies, and sandstorms, there was cholera and thirst,
  But Pharaoh done the best he ever done.
    Down the desert, down the railway, down the river,
      Like Israelites from bondage so he came,
    'Tween the clouds o' dust and fire to the land of his desire,
      And his Moses, it was Sergeant Whatisname!

We are eating dirt in handfuls for to save our daily bread,
  Which we have to buy from those that hate us most,
And we must not raise the money where the Sergeant raised the dead,
  And it's wrong and bad and dangerous to boast.
But he did it on the cheap and on the quiet,
  And he's not allowed to forward any claim—
    Though he drilled a black man white, though he made a mummy fight,
      He will still continue Sergeant Whatisname

Private, Corporal, Colour-Sergeant, and Instructor
But the everlasting miracle's the same!


Our Lady of the Snows

**Canadian Preferential Tariff, 1897**

A nation spoke to a Nation,
   A Queen sent word to a Throne:
"Daughter am I in my mother's house,
   But mistress in my own.
The gates are mine to open,
   As the gates are mine to close,
And I set my house in order,"
   Said our Lady of the Snows.

"Neither with laughter nor weeping,
   Fear or the child's amaze—
Soberly under the White Man's law
   My white men go their ways.
Not for the Gentiles' clamour—
   Insult or threat of blows—
Bow we the knee to Baal,"
   Said our Lady of the Snows.

"My speech is clean and single,
   I talk of common things—
Words of the wharf and the market-place
   And the ware the merchant brings:
Favour to those I favour,
   But a stumbling-block to my foes.
Many there be that hate us,"
   Said our Lady of the Snows.

"I called my chiefs to council
   In the din of a troubled year;
For the sake of a sign ye would not see,
   And a word ye would not hear.
This is our message and answer;
   This is the path we chose:
For we be also a people,"
   Said our Lady of the Snows.

"Carry the word to my sisters—
   To the Queens of the East and the South.
I have proven faith in the Heritage

By more than the word of the mouth.
They that are wise may follow
   Ere the world's war-trumpet blows,,
But I— I am first in the battle,"
   Said our Lady of the Snows.

A Nation spoke to a Nation
   A Throne sent word to a Throne:
"Daughter am I in my mother's house
   But mistress in my own.
The gates are mine to open,
   As the gates are mine to close,
And I abide by my Mother's House,"
   Said our Lady of the Snows.


## Et Dona Ferentes

In extended observation of the ways and works of man,
From the Four-mile Radius roughly to the Plains of Hindustan:
I have drunk with mixed assemblies, seen the racial ruction rise,
And the men of half Creation damning half Creation's eyes.

I have watched them in their tantrums, all that pentecostal crew,
French, Italian, Arab, Spaniard, Dutch and Greek, and Russ and Jew,
Celt and savage, buff and ochre, cream and yellow, mauve and white;
But it never really mattered till the English grew polite;

Till the men with polished toppers, till the men in long frockcoats,
Till the men who do not duel, till the men who war with votes,
Till the breed that take their pleasures as Saint Lawrence took his grid,
Began to "beg your pardon" and—the knowing croupier hid.

Then the bandsmen with their fiddles, and the girls that bring the beer,
Felt the psychologic moment, left the lit casino clear;
But the uninstructed alien, from the Teuton to the Gaul,
Was entrapped, once more, my country, by that suave, deceptive drawl.

As it was in ancient Suez or 'neath wilder, milder skies,
I "observe with apprehension" when the racial ructions rise;
And with keener apprehension, if I read the times aright,
Hear the old casino order: "Watch your man, but be polite.

"Keep your temper. Never answer (that was why they spat and swore).
Don't hit first, but move together (there's no hurry) to the door.
Back to back, and facing outward while the linguist tells 'em how—
"Nous sommes allong ar notre batteau, nous ne voulong pas un row."'

So the hard, pent rage ate inward, till some idiot went too far . . .
"Let'em have it!" and they had it, and the same was merry war.
Fist, umbrella, cane, decanter, lamp and beer-mug, chair and boot—
Till behind the fleeing legions rose the long, hoarse yell for loot.

Then the oil-cloth with its numbers, like a banner fluttered free;
Then the grand piano cantered, on three castors, down the quay;
White, and breathing through their nostrils, silent, systematic, swift—
They removed, effaced, abolished all that man could heave or lift.

Oh, my country, bless the training that from cot to castle runs—
The pitfall of the stranger but the bulwark of thy sons—
Measured speech and ordered action, sluggish soul and unperturbed,
Till we wake our Island-Devil—nowise cool for being curbed!

When the heir of all the ages "has the honour to remain,"
When he will not hear an insult, though men make it ne'er so plain,
When his lips are schooled to meekness. when his back is bowed to blows
Well the keen aas-vogels know it—well the waiting jackal knows.

Build on the flanks of Etna where the sullen smoke-puffs float—
Or bathe in tropic waters where the lean fin dogs the boat—
Cock the gun that is not loaded, cook the frozen dynamite—
But oh, beware my Country, when my Country grows polite!


Kitchener's School

*Being a translation of the song that was made by a Mohammedan school master of Bengal Infantry
(some time on service at Suakim) when he heard that Kitchener was taking money from the English to
build a Madrissa for Hubshees—or a college for the Sudanese.*

Oh hubshee, carry your shoes in your hand and bow your head on your breast!
This is the message of Kitchener who did not break you in jest.
It was permitted to him to fulfil the long-appointed years;
Reaching the end ordained of old over your dead Emirs.

He stamped only before your walls, and the Tomb ye knew was dust:
He gathered up under his armpits all the swords of your trust:
He set a guard on your granaries, securing the weak from the strong:
He said:—"Go work the waterwheels that were abolished so long."

He said:—"Go safely, being abased. I have accomplished my vow.
That was the mercy of Kitchener. Cometh his madness now!
He does not desire as ye desire, nor devise as ye devise:
He is preparing a second host—an army to make you wise.

Not at the mouth of his clean-lipped guns shall ye learn his name again,
But letter by letter, from Kaf to Kaf, at the mouths of his chosen men.
He has gone back to his own city, not seeking presents or bribes,
But openly asking the English for money to buy you Hakims and scribes.

Knowing that ye are forfeit by battle and have no right to live,
He begs for money to bring you learning—and all the English give.
It is their treasure—it is their pleasure—thus are their hearts inclined:
For Allah created the English mad—the maddest of all mankind!

They do not consider the Meaning of Things; they consult not creed nor clan.
Behold, they clap the slave on the back, and behold, he ariseth a man!
They terribly carpet the earth with dead, and before their cannon cool,
They walk unarmed by twos and threes to call the living to school.

How is this reason (which is their reason) to judge a scholar's worth,
By casting a ball at three straight sticks and defending the same with a fourth?
But this they do (which is doubtless a spell) and other matters more strange,
Until, by the operation of years, the hearts of their scholars change:

Till these make come and go great boats or engines upon the rail
(But always the English watch near by to prop them when they fail);
Till these make laws of their own choice and Judges of their own blood;
And all the mad English obey the judges and say that that Law is good.

Certainly they were mad from of old; but I think one new thing,
That the magic whereby they work their magic—wherefrom their fortunes spring—
May be that they show all peoples their magic and ask no price in return.
Wherefore, since ye are bond to that magic, O Hubshee, make haste and learn!

Certainly also is Kitchener mad. But one sure thing I know—
If he who broke you be minded to teach you, to his Madrissa go!
Go, and carry your shoes in your hand and bow your head on your breast,
For he who did not slay you in sport, he will not teach you in jest.

The Young Queen

## The Commonwealth of Australia, inaugurated New Year's Day, 1901

Her hand was still on her sword-hilt, the spur was still on her heel,
She had not cast her harness of grey, war-dinted steel;
High on her red-splashed charger, beautiful, bold, and browned,
Bright-eyed out of the battle, the Young Queen rode to be crowned.

She came to the Old Queen's presence, in the Hall of Our Thousand Years—

In the Hall of the Five Free Nations that are peers among their peers:
Royal she gave the greeting, loyal she bowed the head,
Crying—"Crown me, my Mother!" And the Old Queen rose and said:—

"How can I crown thee further? I know whose standard flies
Where the clean surge takes the Leeuwin or the coral barriers rise.
Blood of our foes on thy bridle, and speech of our friends in thy mouth—
How can I crown thee further, O Queen of the Sovereign South?

"Let the Five Free Nations witness!" But the Young Queen answered swift:—
"It shall be crown of Our crowning to hold Our crown for a gift.
In. the days when Our folk were feeble thy sword made sure Our lands:
Wherefore We come in power to take Our crown at thy hands."

And the Old Queen raised and kissed her, and the jealous circlet prest,
Roped with the pearls of the Northland and red with the gold of the West,
Lit with her land's own opals, levin-hearted, alive,
And the Five-starred Cross above them, for sign of the Nations Five.

So it was done in the Presence—in the Hall of Our Thousand Years,
In the face of the Five Free Nations that have no peer but their peers;
And the Young Queen out of the Southland kneeled down at the Old Queen's knee,
And asked for a mother's blessing on the excellent years to be.

And the Old Queen stooped in the stillness where the jewelled head drooped low:—
"Daughter no more but Sister, and doubly Daughter so—
Mother of many princes—and child of the child I bore,
What good thing shall I wish thee that I have not wished before?

"Shall I give thee delight in dominion—mere pride of thy setting forth?
Nay, we be women together—we know what that lust is worth.
Peace in thy utmost borders, and strength on a road untrod?
These are dealt or diminished at the secret will of God.

"I have swayed troublous councils, I am wise in terrible things;
Father and son and grandson, I have known the hearts of the Kings.
Shall I give thee my sleepless wisdom, or the gift all wisdom above?
Ay, we be women together—I give thee thy people's love:

"Tempered, august, abiding, reluctant of prayers or vows,
Eager in face of peril as thine for thy mother's house.
God requite thee, my Sister, through the excellent years to be,
And make thy people to love thee as thou hast loved me!"

Rimmon

## After Boer War

Duly with knees that feign to quake—
   Bent head and shaded brow—
Yet once again, for my father's sake,
   In Rimmon's House I bow.

The curtains part, the trumpet blares,
   And the eunuchs howl aloud;
And the gilt, swag-bellied idol glares
   Insolent over the crowd.

"This is Rimmon, Lord of the Earth—
   "Fear Him and bow the knee"
And I watch my comrades hide their mirth
   That rode to the wars with me.

For we remember the sun and the sand
   And the rocks whereon we trod,
Ere we came to a scorched and a scornful land
   That did not know our God;

As we remember the sacrifice
   Dead men an hundred laid—
Slain while they served His mysteries,
   And that He would not aid.

Not though we gashed ourselves and wept,
   For the high-priest bade us wait;
Saying He went on a journey or slept,
   Or was drunk or had taken a mate.

(Praise ye Rimmon, King of Kings,
   Who ruleth Earth and Sky!
And again I bow as the censer swings
   And the God Enthroned goes by.)

Ay, we remember His sacred ark
   And the virtuous men that knelt
To the dark and the hush behind the dark
   Wherein we dreamed He dwelt;

Until we entered to hale Him out,
   And found no more than an old
Uncleanly image girded about
   The loins with scarlet and gold.

Him we o'erset with the butts of our spears—

Him and his vast designs—
To be the scorn of our muleteers
   And the jest of our halted lines.

By the picket-pins that the dogs defile,
   In the dung and the dust He lay,
Till the priests ran and chattered awhile
   And wiped Him and took Him away.

Hushing the matter before it was known,
   They returned to our fathers afar,
And hastily set Him afresh on His throne
   Because he had won us the war.

Wherefore with knees that feign to quake—
   Bent head and shaded brow—
To this dead dog, for my father's sake,
   In Rimmon's House I bow!

**Outbreak of Boer War**

"Here is nothing new nor aught unproven," say the Trumpets,
   "Many feet have worn it and the road is old indeed.
"It is the King—the King we schooled aforetime!"
   (Trumpets in the marshes—in the eyot at Runnymede!)

"Here is neither haste, nor hate, nor anger," peal the Trumpets,
   "Pardon for his penitence or pity for his fall.
"It is the King!"— inexorable Trumpets—
   (Trumpets round the scaffold at the dawning by Whitehall!)

"He hath veiled the Crown and hid the Sceptre," warn the Trumpets,
   "He hath changed the fashion of the lies that cloak his will.
"Hard die the Kings—ah hard—dooms hard!" declare the Trumpets,
   Trumpets at the gang-plank where the brawling troop-decks fill!

Ancient and Unteachable, abide—abide the Trumpets!
   Once again the Trumpets, for the shuddering ground-swell brings
Clamour over ocean of the harsh, pursuing Trumpets—
   Trumpets of the Vanguard that have sworn no truce with Kings!

All we have of freedom, all we use or know—
This our fathers bought for us long and long ago.

Ancient Right unnoticed as the breath we draw—
Leave to live by no man's leave, underneath the Law.

Lance and torch and tumult, steel and grey-goose wing
Wrenched it, inch and ell and all, slowly from the King.

Till our fathers 'stablished, after bloody years,
How our King is one with us, first among his peers.

So they bought us freedom—not at little cost
Wherefore must we watch the King, lest our gain be lost,

Over all things certain, this is sure indeed,
Suffer not the old King: for we know the breed.

Give no ear to bondsmen bidding us endure.
Whining "He is weak and far"; crying "Time shall cure.",

(Time himself is witness, till the battle joins,
Deeper strikes the rottenness in the people's loins.)

Give no heed to bondsmen masking war with peace.
Suffer not the old King here or overseas.

They that beg us barter—wait his yielding mood—
Pledge the years we hold in trust—pawn our brother's blood—

Howso' great their clamour, whatsoe'er their claim,
Suffer not the old King under any name!

Here is naught unproven—here is naught to learn.
It is written what shall fall if the King return.

He shall mark our goings, question whence we came,
Set his guards about us, as in Freedom's name.

He shall take a tribute, toll of all our ware;
He shall change our gold for arms—arms we may not bear.

He shall break his judges if they cross his word;
He shall rule above the Law calling on the Lord.

He shall peep and mutter; and the night shall bring
Watchers 'neath our window, lest we mock the King—

Hate and all division; hosts of hurrying spies;
Money poured in secret, carrion breeding flies.

Strangers of his counsel, hirelings of his pay,
These shall deal our Justice: sell—deny—delay.

We shall drink dishonour, we shall eat abuse
For the Land we look to—for the Tongue we use.

We shall take our station, dirt beneath his feet,
While his hired captains jeer us in the street.

Cruel in the shadow, crafty in the sun,
Far beyond his borders shall his teachings run.

Sloven, sullen, savage, secret, uncontrolled,
Laying on a new land evil of the old—

Long-forgotten bondage, dwarfing heart and brain—
All our fathers died to loose he shall bind again.

Here is naught at venture, random nor untrue—
Swings the wheel full-circle, brims the cup anew.

Here is naught unproven, here is nothing hid:
Step for step and word for word—so the old Kings did!

Step by step, and word by word: who is ruled may read.
Suffer not the old Kings: for we know the breed—

All the right they promise—all the wrong they bring.
Stewards of the Judgment, suffer not this King!


Bridge-Guard in the Karroo

"... and will supply details to guard the Blood River Bridge,"
District Orders: Lines of Communication.—South African War.

Sudden the desert changes,
    The raw glare softens and clings,
Till the aching Oudtshoorn ranges
    Stand up like the thrones of Kings—

Ramparts of slaughter and peril—
    Blazing, amazing, aglow—
'Twixt the sky-line's belting beryl
    And the wine-dark flats below.

Royal the pageant closes,

Lit by the last of the sun—
Opal and ash-of-roses,
    Cinnamon, umber, and dun.

The twilight swallows the thicket,
    The starlight reveals the ridge.
The whistle shrills to the picket—
    We are changing guard on the bridge.

(Few, forgotten and lonely,
    Where the empty metals shine—
No, not combatants—only
    Details guarding the line.)

We slip through the broken panel
    Of fence by the ganger's shed;
We drop to the waterless channel
    And the lean track overhead;

We stumble on refuse of rations,
    The beef and the biscuit-tins;
We take our appointed stations,
    And the endless night begins.

We hear the Hottentot herders
    As the sheep click past to the fold—
And the click of the restless girders
    As the steel contracts in the cold—

Voices of jackals calling
    And, loud in the hush between,
A morsel of dry earth falling
    From the flanks of the scarred ravine.

And the solemn firmament marches,
    And the hosts of heaven rise
Framed through the iron arches—
    Banded and barred by the ties,

Till we feel the far track humming,
    And we see her headlight plain,
And we gather and wait her coming—
    The wonderful north-bound train.

(Few, forgotten and lonely,
    Where the white car-windows shine—
No, not combatants—only
    Details guarding the line.)

Quick, ere the gift escape us!
    Out of the darkness we reach
For a handful of week-old papers
    And a mouthful of human speech.

And the monstrous heaven rejoices,
    And the earth allows again,
Meetings, greetings, and voices
    Of women talking with men.

So we return to our places,
    As out on the bridge she rolls;
And the darkness covers our faces,
    And the darkness re-enters our souls.

More than a little lonely
    Where the lessening tail-lights shine.
No—not combatants—only
    Details guarding the line!


The Lesson

**Boer War**

Let us admit it fairly, as a business people should,
We have had no end of a lesson: it will do us no end of good.

Not on a single issue, or in one direction or twain,
But conclusively, comprehensively, and several times and again,
Were all our most holy illusions knocked higher than Gilderoy's kite.
We have had a jolly good lesson, and it serves us jolly well right!

This was not bestowed us under the trees, nor yet in the shade of a tent,
But swingingly, over eleven degrees of a bare brown continent.
From Lamberts to Delagoa Bay, and from Pietersburg to Sutherland,
Fell the phenomenal lesson we learned—with a fulness accorded no other land.

It was our fault, and our very great fault, and not the judgment of Heaven.
We made an Army in our own image, on an island nine by seven,
Which faithfully mirrored its makers' ideals, equipment, and mental attitude—
And so we got our lesson: and we ought to accept it with gratitude.

We have spent two hundred million pounds to prove the fact once more,
That horses are quicker than men afoot, since two and two make four;
And horses have four legs, and men have two legs, and two into four goes twice,

And nothing over except our lesson-and very cheap at the price.

For remember (this our children shall know: we are too near for that knowledge)
Not our mere astonied camps, but Council and Creed and College—
All the obese, unchallenged old things that stifle and overlie us—
Have felt the effects of the lesson we got—an advantage no money could buy us!

Then let us develop this marvellous asset which we alone command,
And which, it may subsequently transpire, will be worth as much as the Rand.
Let us approach this pivotal fact in a humble yet hopeful mood—
We have had no end of a lesson, it will do us no end of good!

It was our fault, and our very great fault—and now we must turn it to use.
We have forty million reasons for failure, but not a single excuse.
So the more we work and the less we talk the better results we shall get—
We have had an Imperial lesson; it may make us an Empire yet!


The Files

**The Sub-editor Speaks**

Files—
The Files—
Office Files!
Oblige me by referring to the Files.
Every question man can raise,
Every phrase of every phase
Of that question is on record in the Files
(Threshed out threadbare fought and finished in the Files).
Ere the Universe at large
Was our new-tipped arrows' targe—
Ere we rediscovered Mammon and his wiles—
Faenza, gentle reader, spent her—five-and-twentieth leader—
(You will find him, and some others, in the Files).
Warn all coming Robert Brownings and Carlyles,
It will interest them to hunt among the Files,
Where unvisited, a-cold,
Lie the crowded years of old
In that Kensall-Green of greatness called the Files
(In our newspaPère-la-Chaise the Office Files),
Where the dead men lay them down
Meekiy sure of long renown,
And above them, sere and swift,
Packs the daily deepening drift
Of the all-recording, all-effacing Files—
The obliterating, automatic Files.

Count the mighty men who slung
Ink, Evangel, Sword, or Tongue
When Reform and you were young—
Made their boasts and spake according in the Files—
(Hear the ghosts that wake applauding in the Files!)
Trace each all-forgot career
From long primer through brevier
Unto Death, a para minion in the Files
(Para minion—solid—bottom of the Files) . . . .
Some successful Kings and Queens adorn the Files.
They were great, their views were leaded,
And their deaths were triple-headed,
So they catch the eye in running through the Files
(Show as blazes in the mazes of the Files);
For their "paramours and priests,"
And their gross, jack-booted feasts,
And their "epoch-marking actions" see the Files.
Was it Bomba fled the blue Sicilian isles?
Was it Saffi, a professor
Once of Oxford, brought redress or
Garibaldi? Who remembers
Forty-odd-year-old Septembers?—
Only sextons paid to dig among the Files
(Such as I am, born and bred among the Files).
You must hack through much deposit
Ere you know for sure who was it
Came to burial with such honour in the Files
(Only seven seasons back beneath the Files).
"Very great our loss and grievous"
So our best and brightest leave us,
"And it ends the Age of Giants," say the Files;
All the '60—'70—'80—'90 Files
(The open-minded, opportunist Files—
The easy "O King, live for ever" Files).
It is good to read a little in the Files;
'Tis a sure and sovereign balm
Unto philosophic calm,
Yea, and philosophic doubt when Life beguiles.
When you know Success is Greatness,
When you marvel at your lateness
In apprehending facts so plain to Smiles
(Self-helpful, wholly strenuous Samuel Smiles).
When your Imp of Blind Desire
Bids you set the Thames afire,
You'll remember men have done so—in the Files.
You'll have seen those flames transpire—in the Files
(More than once that flood has run so—in the Files).
When the Conchimarian horns

Of the reboantic Norns
Usher gentlemen and ladies
With new lights on Heaven and Hades,
Guaranteeing to Eternity
All yesterday's modernity;
When Brocken-spectres made by
Some one's breath on ink parade by,
Very earnest and tremendous,
Let not shows of shows offend us.
When of everything we like we
Shout ecstatic: "Quod ubique,
"Quod ab omnibus means semper!"
Oh, my brother, keep your temper!
Light your pipe and take a look along the Files.
You've a better chance to guess
At the meaning of Success
(Which is Greatness—vide press)
When you've seen it in perspective in the Files.


## The Reformers

Not in the camp his victory lies
    Or triumph in the market-place,
Who is his Nation's sacrifice
    To turn the judgment from his race.

Happy is he who, bred and taught
    By sleek, sufficing Circumstance—
Whose Gospel was the apparelled thoughts
    Whose Gods were Luxury and Chance—

Sees, on the threshold of his days,
    The old life shrivel like a scroll,
And to unheralded dismays
    Submits his body and his soul;

The fatted shows wherein he stood
    Foregoing, and the idiot pride,
That he may prove with his own blood
    All that his easy sires denied—

Ultimate issues, primal springs,
    Demands, abasements, penalties—
The imperishable plinth of things
    Seen and unseen, that touch our peace.

For, though ensnaring ritual dim
   His vision through the after-years,
Yet virtue shall go out of him—
   Example profiting his peers.

With great things charged he shall not hold
   Aloof till great occasion rise,
But serve, full-harnessed, as of old,
   The Days that are the Destinies.

He shall forswear and put away
   The idols of his sheltered house
And to Necessity shall pay
   Unflinching tribute of his vows.

He shall not plead another's act,
   Nor bind him- in another's oath
To weigh the Word above the Fact,
   Or make or take excuse for sloth.

The yoke he bore shall press him still,
   And, long-ingrained effort goad
To find, to fashion, and fulfil
   The cleaner life, the sterner code.

Not in the camp his victory lies—
   The world (unheeding his return)
Shall see it in his children's eyes
   And from his grandson's lips shall learn!


Dirge of Dead Sisters

**For the Nurses who died in the South African War**

Who recalls the twilight and the rangèd tents in order
   (Violet peaks uplifted through the crystal evening air?)
And the clink of iron teacups and the piteous, noble laughter,
   And the faces of the Sisters with the dust upon their hair?

(Now and not hereafter, while the breath is in our nostrils,
   Now and not hereafter, ere the meaner years go by—
Let us now remember many honourable women,
   Such as bade us turn again when we were like to die.)

Who recalls the morning and the thunder through the foothills
   (Tufts of fleecy shrapnel strung along the empty plains?)

And the sun-scarred Red-Cross coaches creeping guarded to the culvert,
    And the faces of the Sisters looking gravely from the trains?

(When the days were torment and the nights were clouded terror,
    When the Powers of Darkness had dominion on our soul—
When we fled consuming through the Seven Hells of Fever,
    These put out their hands to us and healed and made us whole.)

Who recalls the midnight by the bridge's wrecked abutment
    (Autumn rain that rattled like a Maxim on the tin?)
And the lightning-dazzled levels and the streaming, straining wagons,
    And the faces of the Sisters as they bore the wounded in?

(Till the pain was merciful and stunned us into silence—
    When each nerve cried out on God that made the misused clay;
When the Body triumphed and the last poor shame departed—
    These abode our agonies and wiped the sweat away.)

Who recalls the noontide and the funerals through the market
    (Blanket-hidden bodies, flagless, followed by the flies?)
And the footsore firing-party, and the dust and stench and staleness,
    And the faces of the Sisters and the glory in their eyes?

(Bold behind the battle, in the open camp all-hallowed,
    Patient, wise, and mirthful in the ringed and reeking town,
These endured unresting till they rested from their labours—
    Little wasted bodies, ah, so light to lower down!)

Yet their graves are scattered and their names are clean forgotten,
    Earth shall not remember, but the Waiting Angel knows
Them that died at Uitvlugt when the plague was on the city—
    Her that fell at Simon's Town in service on our foes.

Wherefore we they ransomed, while the breath is in our nostrils;
    Now and not hereafter—ere the meaner years go by—
Praise with love and worship many honourable women,
    Those that gave their lives for us when we were like to die!


The Islanders

No doubt but ye are the People—your throne is above the King's.
Whoso speaks in your presence must say acceptable things:
Bowing the head in worship, bending the knee in fear—
Bringing the word well smoothen—such as a King should hear.

Fenced by your careful fathers, ringed by your leaden seas,

Long did ye wake in quiet and long lie down at ease;
Till ye said of Strife, "What is it?" of the Sword, "It is far from our ken":
Till ye made a sport of your shrunken hosts and a toy of your armed men.
Ye stopped your ears to the warning—ye would neither look nor heed—
Ye set your leisure before their toil and your lusts above their need.
Because of your witless learning and your beasts of warren and chase,
Ye grudged your sons to their service and your fields for their camping-place.
Ye forced them to glean in the highways the straw for the bricks they brought;
Ye forced them follow in byways the craft that ye never taught.
Ye hindered and hampered and crippled; ye thrust out of sight and away
Those that would serve you for honour and those that served you for pay.
Then were the judgments loosened; then was your shame revealed,
At the hands of a little people, few but apt in the field.
Yet ye were saved by a remnant (and your land's long-suffering star),
When your strong men cheered in their millions while your striplings went to the war.
Sons of the sheltered city—unmade, unhandled, unmeet—
Ye pushed them raw to the battle as ye picked them raw from the street.
And what did ye look they should compass? Warcraft learned in a breath,
Knowledge unto occasion at the first far view of Death?
So? And ye train your horses and the dogs ye feed and prize?
How are the beasts more worthy than the souls, your sacrifice?
But ye said, "Their valour shall show them"; but ye said, "The end is close."
And ye sent them comfits and pictures to help them harry your foes:
And ye vaunted your fathomless power, and ye flaunted your iron pride,
Ere—ye fawned on the Younger Nations for the men who could shoot and ride!
Then ye returned to your trinkets; then ye contented your souls
With the flannelled fools at the wicket or the muddied oafs at the goals.
Given to strong delusion, wholly believing a lie,
Ye saw that the land lay fenceless, and ye let the months go by
Waiting some easy wonder, hoping some saving sign
Idle—openly idle—in the lee of the forespent Line.
Idle—except for your boasting—and what is your boasting worth
If ye grudge a year of service to the lordliest life on earth?
Ancient, effortless, ordered, cycle on cycle set,
Life so long untroubled, that ye who inherit forget
It was not made with the mountains, it is not one with the deep.
Men, not gods, devised it. Men, not gods, must keep.
Men, not children, servants, or kinsfolk called from afar,
But each man born in the Island broke to the matter of war.
Soberly and by custom taken and trained for the same,
Each man born in the Island entered at youth to the game—
As it were almost cricket, not to be mastered in haste,
But after trial and labour, by temperance, living chaste.
As it were almost cricket—as it were even your play,
Weighed and pondered and worshipped, and practised day and day.
So ye shall bide sure-guarded when the restless lightnings wake
In the womb of the blotting war-cloud, and the pallid nations quake.
So, at the haggard trumpets, instant your soul shall leap

Forthright, accoutred, accepting—alert from the wells of sleep.
So at the threat ye shall summon—so at the need ye shall send
Men, not children or servants, tempered and taught to the end;
Cleansed of servile panic, slow to dread or despise,
Humble because of knowledge, mighty by sacrifice.
But ye say, "It will mar our comfort." Ye say, "It will minish our trade."
Do ye wait for the spattered shrapnel ere ye learn how a gun is laid?
For the low, red glare to southward when the raided coast-towns burn?
(Light ye shall have on that lesson, but little time to learn.)
Will ye pitch some white pavilion, and lustily even the odds,
With nets and hoops and mallets, with rackets and bats and rods?
Will the rabbit war with your foemen—the red deer horn them for hire?
Your kept cock—pheasant keep you?—he is master of many a shire.
Arid, aloof, incurious, unthinking, unthanking, gelt,
Will ye loose your schools to flout them till their brow-beat columns melt?
Will ye pray them or preach them, or print them, or ballot them back from your shore?
Will your workmen issue a mandate to bid them strike no more?
Will ye rise and dethrone your rulers? (Because ye were idle both?
Pride by Insolence chastened? Indolence purged by Sloth?)
No doubt but ye are the People; who shall make you afraid?
Also your gods are many; no doubt but your gods shall aid.
Idols of greasy altars built for the body's ease;
Proud little brazen Baals and talking fetishes;
Teraphs of sept and party and wise wood-pavement gods—
These shall come down to the battle and snatch you from under the rods?
From the gusty, flickering gun-roll with viewless salvoes rent,
And the pitted hail of the bullets that tell not whence they were sent.
When ye are ringed as with iron, when ye are scourged as with whips,
When the meat is yet in your belly, and the boast is yet on your lips;
When ye go forth at morning and the noon beholds you broke,
Ere ye lie down at even, your remnant, under the yoke?

No doubt but ye are the People—absolute, strong, and wise;
Whatever your heart has desired ye have not withheld from your eyes.
On your own heads, in your own hands, the sin and the saving lies!


The Peace of Dives


The word came down to Dives in Torment where he lay:
"Our World is full of wickedness, My Children maim and slay,
   "And the Saint and Seer and Prophet
   "Can make no better of it
"Than to sanctify and prophesy and pray.

"Rise up, rise up, thou Dives, and take again thy gold,
"And thy women and thy housen as they were to thee of old.

“It may be grace hath found thee
“In the furnace where We bound thee,
And that thou shalt bring the peace My Son foretold.”

Then merrily rose Dives and leaped from out his fire,
And walked abroad with diligence to do the Lord's desire;
    And anon the battles ceased,
    And the captives were released,
And Earth had rest from Goshen to Gadire,

The Word came down to Satan that raged and roared alone,'
'Mid the shouting of the peoples by the cannon overthrown
    (But the Prophets, Saints, and Seers
    Set each other by the ears,
For each would claim the marvel as his own):

“Rise up, rise up, thou Satan, upon the Earth to go,
“And prove the Peace of Dives if it be good or no:
    “For all that he hath planned
    “We deliver to thy hand,
“As thy skill shall serve, to break it or bring low.”

Then mightily rose Satan, and about the Earth he hied,
And breathed on Kings in idleness and Princes drunk with pride.
    But for all the wrong he breathed
    There was never sword unsheathed,
And the fires he lighted flickered out and died.

Then terribly rose Satan, and he darkened Earth afar,
Till he came on cunning Dives where the money-changers are;
    And he saw men pledge their gear
    For the gold that buys the spear,
And the helmet and the habergeon of war.

Yea to Dives came the Persian and the Syrian and the Mede—
their hearts were nothing altered, nor their cunning nor their greed—
    And they pledged their flocks and farms
    For the King compelling arms,
And Dives lent according to their need,

Then Satan said to Dives:—”Return again with me,
“Who hast broken His Commandment in the day He set thee free,
    “Who grindest for thy greed,
    “Man's belly-pinch and need;
“And the blood of Man to filthy usury!”

Then softly answered Dives where the money-changers sit:—
“My refuge is Our Master, O My Master in the Pit.

"But behold all Earth is laid
"In the Peace which I have made,
"And behold I wait on thee to trouble it!"

Then angrily turned Satan, and about the Seas he fled,
To shake the new-sown peoples with insult, doubt, and dread;
    But, for all the sleight he used,
    There was never squadron loosed.
And the brands he flung flew dying and fell dead.

But to Dives came Atlantis and the Captains of the West—
And their hates were nothing weakened nor their anger nor unrest—
    And they pawned their utmost trade
    For the dry, decreeing blade;
And Dives lent and took of them their best.

Then Satan said to Dives:—"Declare thou by The Name,
"The secret of thy subtlety that turneth mine to shame.
    "It is known through all the Hells
    "How my peoples mocked my spells,
"And my faithless Kings denied me ere I came."

Then answered cunning Dives: "Do not gold and hate abide
"At the heart of every Magic, yea, and senseless fear beside?
    "With gold and fear and hate
    "I have harnessed state to state,
"And by hate and fear and gold their hates are tied.

"For hate men seek a weapon, for fear they seek a shield—
" Keener blades and broader targes than their frantic neighhours wield—
    "For gold I arm their hands,
    "And for gold I buy their lands,
"And for gold I sell their enemies the yield.

"Their nearest foes may purchase, or their furthest friends may lease,
"One by one from Ancient Accad to the Islands of the Seas.
    "And their covenants they make
    "For the naked iron's sake,
"But I— I trap them armoured into peace.

"The flocks that Egypt pledged me to Assyria I drave,
"And Pharaoh hath the increase of the herds that Sargon gave.
    "Not for Ashdod overthrown
    "Will the Kings destroy their own,
"Or their peoples wake the strife they feign to brave.

"Is not Carchernish like Calno? For the steeds of their desire
"They have sold me seven harvests that I sell to Crowning Tyre;

"And the Tyrian sweeps the plains
    "With a thousand hired wains,
"And the Cities keep the peace and—share the hire.

"Hast thou seen the pride of Moab? For the swords about his path,
"His bond is to Philistia, in half of all he hath.
    "And he dare not draw the sword
    "Till Gaza give the word,
"And he show release from Askalon and Gath,

"Wilt thou call again thy peoples, wilt thou craze anew thy Kings?
"Lo! my lightnings pass before thee, and their whistling servant brings,
    "Ere the drowsy street hath stirred—
    "Every masked and midnight word,
"And the nations break their fast upon these things.

"So I make a jest of Wonder, and a mock of Time and Space.
"The roofless Seas an hostel, and the Earth a market-place,
    "Where the anxious traders know
    "Each is surety for his foe,
"And none may thrive without his fellows' grace.

"Now this is all my subtlety and this is all my wit,
"God give thee good enlightenment, My Master in the Pit.
    "But behold all Earth is laid
    "In the Peace which I have made,
"And behold I wait on thee to trouble it!"


South Africa

Lived a woman wonderful,
    (May the Lord amend her!)
Neither simple, kind, nor true,
But her Pagan beauty drew
Christian gentlemen a few
    Hotly to attend her.

Christian gentlemen a few
    From Berwick unto Dover;
For she was South Africa,
And she was South Africa,
She was Our South Africa,
    Africa all over!

Half her land was dead with drouth,
    Half was red with battle;

She was fenced with fire and sword
Plague on pestilence outpoured,
Locusts on the greening sward
   And murrain on the cattle!

True, ah true, and overtrue.
   That is why we love her!
For she is South Africa,
And she is South Africa,
She is Our South Africa,
   Africa all over!

Bitter hard her lovers toiled,
   Scandalous their payment,
Food forgot on trains derailed;
Cattle-dung where fuel failed;
Water where the mules had staled;
   And sackcloth for their raiment!

So she filled their mouths with dust
   And their bones with fever;
Greeted them with cruel lies;
Treated them despiteful-wise;
Meted them calamities
   Till they vowed to leave her!

They took ship and they took sail,
   Raging, from her borders
In a little, none the less,
They forgat their sore duresse,
They forgave her waywardness
   And returned for orders!

They esteemed her favour more
   Than a Throne's foundation.
For the glory of her face
Bade farewell to breed and race
Yea, and made their burial-place
   Altar of a Nation!

Wherefore, being bought by blood,
   And by blood restored
To the arms that nearly lost,
She, because of all she cost,
Stands, a very woman, most
   Perfect and adored!

On your feet, and let them know

This is why we love her!
For she is South Africa,
She is Our South Africa,
Is Our Own South Africa,
    Africa all over!


## The Settler

South African War ended, May, 1902

Here, where my fresh-turned furrows run,
    And the deep soil glistens red,
I will repair the wrong that was done
    To the living and the dead.
Here, where the senseless bullet fell,
    And the barren shrapnel burst,
I will plant a tree, I will dig a well,
    Against the heat and the thirst.

Here, in a large and a sunlit land,
    Where no wrong bites to the bone,
I will lay my hand in my neighbour's hand,
    And together we will atone
For the set folly and the red breach
    And the black waste of it all;
Giving and taking counsel each
    Over the cattle-kraal.

Here will we join against our foes—
    The hailstroke and the storm,
And the red and rustling cloud that blows
    The locust's mile-deep swarm.
Frost and murrain and floods let loose
    Shall launch us side by side
In the holy wars that have no truce
    'Twixt seed and harvest-tide.

Earth, where we rode to slay or be slain,
    Our love shall redeem unto life.
We will gather and lead to her lips again
    The waters of ancient strife,
From the far and fiercely guarded streams
    And the pools where we lay in wait,
Till the corn cover our evil dreams
    And the young corn our hate.

And when we bring old fights to mind,
    We will not remember the sin—
If there be blood on his head of my kind,
    Or blood on my head of his kin—
For the ungrazed upland, the untilled lea
    Crk, and the fields forlorn:
"The dead must bury their dead, but ye—
    Ye serve an host unborn."

Bless then, Our God, the new-yoked plough
    And the good beasts that draw,
And the bread we eat in the sweat of our brow
    According to Thy Law.
After us cometh a multitude—
    Prosper the work of our hands,
That we may feed with our land's food
    The folk of all our lands!

Here, in the waves and the troughs of the plains,
    Where the healing stillness lies,
And the vast, benignant sky restrains
    And the long days make wise—
Bless to our use the rain and the sun
    And the blind seed in its bed,
That we may repair the wrong that was done
    To the living and the dead!


Chant-Pagan

**English Irregular discharged**

Me that 'ave been what I've been—
    Me that 'ave gone where I've gone—
Me that 'ave seen what I've seen—
    'Ow can I ever take on
With awful old England again,
An' 'ouses both sides of the street,
And 'edges two sides of the lane,
And the parson an' gentry between,
An' touchin' my 'at when we meet—
Me that 'ave been what I've been?

Me that 'ave watched 'arf a world
'Eave up all shiny with dew,
Kopje on kop to the sun,
An' as soon as the mist let 'em through

Our 'elios winkin' like fun—
Three sides of a ninety-mile square,
Over valleys as big as a shire—
Are ye there? Are ye there? Are ye there?
An' then the blind drum of our fire . . .
An' I'm rollin' 'is lawns for the Squire,
      Me!

Me that 'ave rode through the dark
Forty mile, often, on end,
Along the Ma'ollisberg Range,
With only the stars for my mark
An' only the night for my friend,
An' things runnin' off as you pass,
An' things jumpin' up in the grass,
An' the silence, the shine an' the size
Of the 'igh, unexpressible skies—
I am takin' some letters almost
As much as a mile to the post,
An' "mind you come back with the change"!
      Me!

Me that saw Barberton took
When we dropped through the clouds on their 'ead,
An' they 'ove the guns over and fled
Me that was through Di'mond 'ill,
An' Pieters an' Springs an' Belfast—
From Dundee to Vereeniging all—
Me that stuck out to the last
(An' five bloomin' bars on my chest)—
I am doin' my Sunday-school best,
By the 'elp of the Squire an' 'is wife
(Not to mention the 'ousemaid an' cook),
To come in an' 'ands up an' be still,
An' honestly work for my bread,
My livin' in that state of life
To which it shall please God to call
      Me!

Me that 'ave followed my trade
In the place where the Lightnin's are made,
'Twixt the Rains and the Sun and the Moon—
Me that lay down an' got up
Three years with the sky for my roof—
That 'ave ridden my 'unger an' thirst
Six thousand raw mile on the hoof,
With the Vaal and the Orange for cup,
An' the Brandwater Basin for dish—

Oh! it's 'ard to be'ave as they wish
(Too 'ard, an' a little too soon),
I'll 'ave to think over it first—
        Me!

I will arise an' get 'ence;—
I will trek South and make sure
If it's only my fancy or not
That the sunshine of England is pale,
And the breezes of England are stale,
An' there's somethin' gone small with the lot;
For I know of a sun an' a wind,
An' some plains and a mountain be'ind,
An' some graves by a barb-wire fence;
An' a Dutchman I've fought 'oo might give
Me a job were I ever inclined,
To look in an' offsaddle an' live
Where there's neither a road nor a tree—
But only my Maker an' me,
And I think it will kill me or cure,
So I think I will go there an' see.
        Me!

M.I.

**Mounted Infantry of the Line**

I wish my mother could see me now, with a fence-post under my arm,
And a knife and a spoon in my putties that I found on a Boer farm,
Atop of a sore-backed Argentine, with a thirst that you could n't buy.
   I used to be in the Yorkshires once
   (Sussex, Lincolns, and Rifles once),
   Hampshires, Glosters, and Scottish once! (ad lib.)
       But now I am M.I.

That is what we are known as—that is the name you must call
If you want officers' servants, pickets an' 'orseguards an' all—
Details for buryin'-parties, company-cooks or supply—
Turn out the chronic Ikonas! Roll up the—* M.I.!

My 'ands are spotty with veldt-sores, my shirt is a button an' frill,
An' the things I've used my bay'nit for would make a tinker ill!
An' I don't know whose dam' column I'm in, nor where we're trekkin' nor why.
   I've trekked from the Vaal to the Orange once—
   From the Vaal to the greasy Pongolo once—
   (Or else it was called the Zambesi once)—

For now I am M.I.

That is what we are known as-we are the push you require
For outposts all night under freezin', an' rearguard all day under fire.
Anything 'ot or unwholesome? Anything dusty or dry?
Borrow a bunch of Ikonas! Trot out the—M.I.!

Our Sergeant-Major's a subaltern, our Captain's a Fusilier—
Our Adjutant's "late of Somebody's 'Orse," an' a Melbourne auctioneer;
But you couldn't spot us at 'arf a mile from the crackest caval-ry.
   They used to talk about Lancers once,
   Hussars, Dragoons, an' Lancers once,
   'Elmets, pistols, an' carbines once,
       But now we are M.I.!

That is what we are known as—we are the orphans they blame
For beggin' the loan of an 'ead-stall an' makin' a mount to the same.
'Can't even look at their 'orselines but some one goes bellerin' "Hi!
"'Ere comes a burglin' Ikona!" Footsack you—M.I.!

We're trekkin' our twenty miles a day an' bein' loved by the Dutch,
But we don't hold on by the mane no more, nor lose our stirrups—much;
An' we scout with a senior man in charge where the 'oly white flags fly.
   We used to think they were friendly once,
   Didn't take any precautions once
   (Once, my ducky, an' only once!)
       But now we are M.I.!

That is what we are known as—we are the beggars that got
Three days "to learn equitation," an' six months o' bloomin' well trot!
Cow-guns, an' cattle, an' convoys—an' Mister De Wet on the fly—
We are the rollin' Ikonas! We are the—M.I.

The new fat regiments come from home, imaginin' vain V. C.'s
(The same as your talky-fighty men which are often Number Threes),
But our words o' command are "Scatter" an' "Close" an' "Let your wounded lie."
   We used to rescue 'em noble once—
   Givin' the range as we raised 'em once,
   Gettin' 'em killed as we saved 'em once—
       But now we are M.I.

That is what we are known as—we are the lanterns you view
After a fight round the kopjes, lookin' for men that we knew;
Whistlin' an' callin' together, 'altin' to catch the reply:—
"'Elp me! O 'elp me, Ikonas! This way, the—M.I.!"

I wish my mother could see me now, a-gatherin' news on my own,
When I ride like a General up to the scrub and ride back like Tod Sloan,

Remarkable close to my 'orse's neck to let the shots go by.
   We used to fancy it risky once
   (Called it a reconnaissance once),
   Under the charge of an orf'cer once,
       But now we are M.I.!

That is what we are known as—that is the song you must say
When you want men to be Mausered at one and a penny a day;
We are no five-bob Colonials—we are the 'ome-made supply,
Ask for the London Ikonas! Ring up the—M.I.!

I wish myself could talk to myself as I left 'im a year ago;
I could tell 'im a lot that would save 'im a lot on the things that 'e ought to know!
When I think o' that ignorant barrack-bird, it almost makes me cry.
   I used to belong in an Army once
   (Gawd! what a rum little Army once),
   Red little, dead little Army once!
       But now I am M.I.!

That is what we are known as—we are the men that have been
Over a year at the business, smelt it an' felt it an' seen.
We 'ave got 'old of the needful—you will be told by and by;
Wait till you've 'eard the Ikonas, spoke to the old M.I.!

Mount—march, Ikonas! Stand to your 'orses again!
Mop off the frost on the saddles, mop up the miles on the plain.
Out go the stars in the dawnin', up goes our dust to the sky,
Walk—trot, Ikonas! Trek jou the old M.I.!

*Number according to taste and service of audience.*

Columns

**Mobile Columns of the Boer War**

Out o' the wilderness, dusty an' dry
   (Time, an' 'igh time to be trekkin' again!)
'Oo is it 'eads to the Detail Supply?
   A section, a pompom, an' six 'undred men.

'Ere comes the clerk with 'is lantern an' keys
   (Time, an' 'igh time to be trekkin' again!)
"Surplus of everything—draw what you please
   "For the section, the pompom, an' six 'undred men."

"What are our orders an' where do we lay?"

(Time, an' 'igh time to be trekkin' again!)
"You came after dark—you will leave before day,
   "You section, you pompom, you six 'undred men!"

Down the tin street, 'alf awake an' unfed,
'Ark to 'em blessin' the Gen'ral in bed!

Now by the church an' the outspan they wind—
Over the ridge an' it's all lef' be'ind
   For the section, etc.

Soon they will camp as the dawn's growin' grey.
Roll up for coffee an' sleep while they may—
   The section, etc.

Read their 'ome letters, their papers an' such,
For they'll move after dark to astonish the Dutch
   With a section, etc.

'Untin' for shade as the long hours pass—
Blankets on rifles or burrows in grass,
   Lies the section, etc.

Dossin' or beatin' a shirt in the sun,
Watching chameleons or cleanin' a gun,
   Waits the section, etc.

With nothin' but stillness as far as you please,
An' the silly mirage stringin' islands an' seas
   Round the section, etc.

So they strips off their hide an' they grills in their bones,
Till the shadows crawl out from beneath the pore stones
   Towards the section, etc.

An' the Mauser-bird stops an' the jackals begin,
An' the 'orse-guard comes up and the Gunners 'ook in
   As a 'int to the pompom an' six 'undred men . . . .

Off through the dark with the stars to rely on—
(Alpha Centauri an' somethin' Orion)
   Moves the section, etc.

Same bloomin' 'ole which the ant-bear 'as broke,
Same bloomin' stumble an' same bloomin' joke
   Down the section, etc.

Same "which is right?" where the cart-tracks divide,

Same "give it up" from the same clever guide
    To the section, etc.

Same tumble-down on the same 'idden farm,
Same white-eyed Kaffir 'oo gives the alarm
    Of the section, etc.

Same shootin' wild at the end o' the night,
Same flyin'-tackle an' same messy fight,
    By the section, etc.

Same ugly 'iccup an' same 'orrid squeal,
When it's too dark to see an' it's too late to feel
    In the section, etc.

(Same batch of prisoners, 'airy an' still,
Watchin' their comrades bolt over the 'ill
    From the section, etc.)

Same chilly glare in the eye of the sun
As 'e gets up displeasured to see what was done
    By the section, etc,

Same splash o' pink on the stoep or the kraal,
An' the same quiet face which 'as finished with all
    In the section, the pompom, an' six 'undred men.

Out o' the wilderness, dusty an' dry
    (Time, an' 'igh time to be trekkin' again!)
'Oo is it 'eads to the Detail Supply?
    A section, a pompom, an' six 'undred men.


The Parting of the Columns

" . . . On the —th instant a mixed detachment of Colonials left—for Cape Town, there to rejoin their respective homeward-bound contingents, after (fifteen months' service in the field. They were escorted to the station by the regular troops in garrison and the bulk of Colonel—'s column, which has just come in to refit, preparatory to further operations. The leave-taking was of the most cordial character, the men cheering each other continuously.
— Any Newspaper, during the South African War.

We've rode and fought and ate and drunk as rations* come to hand,
Together for a year and more around this stinkin' land:
Now you are goin' home again, but we must see it through.
We needn't tell we liked you well. Good-bye—good luck to you!

You 'ad no special call to come, and so you doubled out,
And learned us how to camp and cook an' steal a horse and scout.
Whatever game we fancied most, you joyful played it too,
And rather better on the whole. Good-bye—good luck to you!

There isn't much we 'ave n't shared, since Kruger cut and run,
The same old work the same old skoff the same old dust and sun;
The same old chance that laid us out, or winked an' let us through;
The same old Life, the same old Death. Good-bye—good luck to you!

Our blood 'as truly mixed with yours—all down the Red Cross train.
We've bit the same thermometer in Bloeming-typhoidtein.**
We've 'ad the same old temp'rature—the same relapses too,
The same old saw-backed fever-chart. Good-bye—good luck to you!

But 'twasn't merely this an' that (which all the world may know),
'Twas how you talked an' looked at things which made us like you so.
All independent, queer an' odd, but most amazin' new,
My word! you shook us up to rights. Good-bye—good luck to you!

Think o' the stories round the fire, the tales along the trek—
O' Calgary an' Wellin'ton, an' Sydney and Quebec;
Of mine an' farm, an' ranch an' run, an' moose an' cariboo,
An' parrots peckin' lambs to death! Good-bye—good luck to you!

We've seen your 'ome by word o' mouth, we've watched your rivers shine,
We've 'eard your bloomin' forests blow of eucalip' and pine;
Your young, gay countries north and south, we feel we own 'em too,
For they was made by rank an' file. Good-bye—good luck to you,

We'll never read the papers now without inquirin' first
For word from all those friendly dorps where you was born an' nursed.
Why, Dawson, Galle, an' Montreal—Port Darwin—Timaru,
They're only just across the road! Good-bye—good luck to you!

Good-bye!—So—long! Don't lose yourselves—nor us, nor all kind friends,
But tell the girls your side the drift we're comin'— when it ends!
Good-bye, you bloomin' Atlases! You've taught us somethin' new:
The world's no bigger than a kraal. Good-bye—good luck to you!

*Convoys were not seldom captured by the Boers.
**There were several thousands of typhoid cases at Bloemfontein. Hence its name among the troops.


Two Kopjes

**Made Yeomanry towards End of Boer War**

Only two African kopjes,
    Only the cart-tracks that wind
Empty and open between 'em,
    Only the Transvaal behind;
Only an Aldershot column
    Marching to conquer the land . . . .
Only a sudden and solemn
    Visit, unarmed, to the Rand.

Then scorn not the African kopje,
    The kopje that smiles in the heat,
The wholly unoccupied kopje,
    The home of Cornelius and Piet.
You can never be sure of your kopje,
    But of this be you blooming well sure,
A kopje is always a kopje,
    And a Boojer is always a Boer!

Only two African kopjes,
    Only the vultures above,
Only baboons—at the bottom,
    Only some buck on the move;
Only a Kensington draper
    Only pretending to scout . . . .
Only bad news for the paper,
    Only another knock-out.

Then mock not the African kopje,
    And rub not your flank on its side,
The silent and simmering kopje,
    The kopje beloved by the guide.
You can never be sure of your kopje,
    But of this be you blooming well sure,
A kopje is always a kopje,
    And a Boojer is always a Boer!

Only two African kopjes,
    Only the dust of their wheels,
Only a bolted commando,
    Only our guns at their heels . . . .
Only a little barb-wire,
    Only a natural fort,
Only "by sections retire,"
    Only "regret to report!"

Then mock not the African kopje.
    Especially when it is twins,

One sharp and one table-topped kopje
  For that's where the trouble begins.
You can never be sure of your kopje,
  But of this be you blooming well sure,
A kopje is always a kopje,
  And a Boojer is always a Boer!

Only two African kopjes .
  Baited the same as before—
Only we've had it so often,
  Only we're taking no more . . . .
Only a wave to our troopers,
  Only our flanks swinging past,
Only a dozen voorloopers,

  Only we've learned it at last!
Then mock not the African kopje,
  But take off your hat to the same,
The patient, impartial old kopje,
  The kopje that taught us the game!
For all that we knew in the Columns,
  And all they've forgot on the Staff,
We learned at the Fight o' Two Kopjes,
  Which lasted two years an' a half,

O mock not the African kopje,
  Not even when peace has been signed—
The kopje that isn't a kopje—
  The kopje that copies its kind.
You can never be sure of your kopje,
  But of this be you blooming well sure,
That a kopje is always a kopje,
  And a Boojer is always a Boer!


The Instructor

**Non-commissioned Officers of the Line**

At times when under cover I 'ave said,
To keep my spirits up an' raise a laugh,
'Earin 'im pass so busy over-'ead—
Old Nickel-Neck, 'oo is n't on the Staff—
"There's one above is greater than us all."

Before 'im I 'ave seen my Colonel fall,
An' watched 'im write my Captain's epitaph,

So that a long way off it could be read—
He 'as the knack o' makin' men feel small—
Old Whistle Tip, 'oo is n't on the Staff.

There is no sense in fleein' (I 'ave fled),
Better go on an' do the belly-crawl,
An' 'ope 'e 'll 'it some other man instead
Of you 'e seems to 'unt so speshual—
Fitzy van Spitz, 'oo is n't on the Staff.

An' thus in mem'ry's cinematograph,
Now that the show is over, I recall
The peevish voice an' 'oary mushroom 'ead
Of 'im we owned was greater than us all,
'Oo give instruction to the quick an' the dead—
The Shudderin' Beggar—not upon the Staff!


Boots

**Infantry Columns**

We're foot—slog—slog—slog—sloggin' over Africa
Foot—foot—foot—foot—sloggin' over Africa—
(Boots—boots—boots—boots—movin' up and down again!)
        There's no discharge in the war!

Seven—six—eleven—five—nine-an'-twenty mile today—
Four—eleven—seventeen—thirty—two the day before—
(Boots—boots—boots—boots—movin' up and down again!)
        There's no discharge in the war!

Don't—don't—don't—don't—look at what's in front of you.
(Boots—boots—boots—boots—movin' up an' down again);
Men—men—men—men—men go mad with watchin' 'em,
        An' there's no discharge in the war!

Try—try—try—try—to think o' something different—
Oh—my—God—keep—me from goin' lunatic!
(Boots—boots—boots—boots—movin' up an' down again!)
        There's no discharge in the war!

Count—count—count—count—the bullets in the bandoliers.
If—your—eyes—drop—they will get atop o' you
(Boots—boots—boots—boots—movin' up and down again)—
        There's no discharge in the war!

We—can—stick—out—'unger, thirst, an' weariness,
But—not-— not—not—not the chronic sight of 'em—
Boots—boots—boots—boots—movin' up an' down again,
        An' there's no discharge in the war!

'Tain't—so—bad—by—day because o' company,
But—night—brings—long—strings—o' forty thousand million
Boots—boots—boots—boots—movin' up an' down again.
        There's no discharge in the war!

I—'ave—marched—six—weeks in 'Ell an' certify
It—is—not—fire—devils—dark or anything,
But boots—boots—boots—boots—movin' up an' down again,
        An' there's no discharge in the war!

## The Married Man

### Reservist of the Line

The bachelor 'e fights for one
   As joyful as can be;
But the married man don't call it fun,
   Because 'e fights for three—
For 'Im an' 'Er an' It
   (An' Two an' One make Three)
'E wants to finish 'is little bit,
   An' 'e wants to go 'ome to 'is tea!

The bachelor pokes up 'is 'ead
   To see if you are gone;
But the married man lies down instead,
   An' waits till the sights come on,
For 'Im an' 'Er an' a hit
   (Direct or ricochee)
'E wants to finish 'is little bit,
   An' 'e wants to go 'ome to 'is tea.

The bachelor will miss you clear
   To fight another day;
But the married man, 'e says "No fear!"
   'E wants you out of the way
Of 'Im an' 'Er an' It
   (An' 'is road to 'is farm or the sea),
'E wants to finish 'is little bit,
   An' 'e wants to go 'ome to 'is tea.

The bachelor 'e fights 'is fight
   An' stretches out an' snores;
But the married man sits up all night—
   For 'e don't like out-o'-doors.
'E'll strain an' listen an' peer
   An' give the first alarm—
For the sake o' the breathin' 'e's used to 'ear
   An' the 'ead on the thick of 'is arm.

The bachelor may risk 'is 'ide
   To 'elp you when you're downed;
But the married man will wait beside
   Till the ambulance comes round.
'E'll take your 'ome address
   An' all you've time to say,
Or if 'e sees there's 'ope, 'e'll press
   Your art'ry 'alf the day—

For 'Im an' 'Er an' It
   (An' One from Three leaves Two),
For 'e knows you wanted to finish your bit,
   An' 'e knows 'oo's wantin' you.
Yes, 'Im an' 'Er an' It
   (Our 'oly One in Three),
We're all of us anxious, to finish our bit,
   An' we want to get 'ome to our tea!

Yes, It an' 'Er an' 'Im,
   Which often makes me think
The married man must sink or swim
   An'—'e can't afford to sink!
Oh 'Im an' It an' 'Er
   Since Adam an' Eve began!
So I'd rather fight with the bacheler
   An' be nursed by the married man!

Lichtenberg

**New South Wales Contingent**

Smells are surer than sounds or sights
   To make your heart-strings crack—
They start those awful voices o' nights
   That whisper, "Old man, come back!"
That must be why the big things pass
   And the little things remain,

Like the smell of the wattle by Lichtenberg,
    Riding in, in the rain.

There was some silly fire on the flank
    And the small wet drizzling down
There were the sold-out shops and the bank
    And the wet, wide-open town;
And we were doing escort-duty
    To somebody's baggage-train,
And I smelt wattle by Lichtenberg—
    Riding in, in the rain.

It was all Australia to me—
    All I had found or missed:
Every face I was crazy to see,
    And every woman I'd kissed:
All that I should n't ha' done, God knows!
    (As He knows I'll do it again),
That smell of the wattle round Lichtenberg,
    Riding in, in the rain!

And I saw Sydney the same as ever,
    The picnics and brass-bands;
And my little homestead on Hunter River
    And my new vines joining hands.
It all came over me in one act
    Quick as a shot through the brain—
With the smell of the wattle round Lichtenberg,
    Riding in, in the rain.

I have forgotten a hundred fights,
    But one I shall not forget—
With the raindrops bunging up my sights
    And my eyes bunged up with wet;
And through the crack and the stink of the cordite
    (Ah Christ! My country again!)
The smell of the wattle by Lichtenberg,
    Riding in, in the rain!

Stellenbosh

**Composite Columns**

The general 'eard the firin' on the flank,
    An' 'e sent a mounted man to bring 'im back
The silly, pushin' person's name an' rank

'Oo'd dared to answer Brother Boer's attack:
For there might 'ave been a serious engagement,
   An' 'e might 'ave wasted 'alf a dozen men;
So 'e ordered 'im to stop 'is operations round the kopjes,
   An' 'e told 'im off before the Staff at ten!

And it all goes into the laundry,
But it never comes out in the wash,
'Ow we're sugared about by the old men
('Eavy sterned amateur old men!)
That 'amper an' 'inder an' scold men
For fear o' Stellenbosh!*

The General 'ad "produced a great effect,"
   The General 'ad the country cleared—almost;
The General "'ad no reason to expect,"
   And the Boers 'ad us bloomin' well on toast!
For we might 'ave crossed the drift before the twilight,
   Instead o' sitting down an' takin' root;
But we was not allowed, so the Boojers scooped the crowd,
   To the last survivin' bandolier an' boot.

The General saw the farm'ouse in 'is rear,
   With its stoep so nicely shaded from the sun;
Sez 'e, "I'll pitch my tabernacle 'ere,"
   An' 'e kept us muckin' round till 'e 'ad done.
For 'e might 'ave caught the confluent pneumonia
   From sleepin' in his gaiters in the dew;
So 'e took a book an' dozed while the other columns closed
   And De Wet's commando out an' trickled through!

The General saw the mountain-range ahead,
   With their 'elios showin' saucy on the 'eight,
So 'e 'eld us to the level ground instead,
   An' telegraphed the Boojers would n't fight.
For 'e might 'ave gone an' sprayed 'em with a pompom,
   Or 'e might 'ave slung a squadron out to see—
But 'e was n't takin' chances in them 'igh an' 'ostile kranzes—
   He was markin' time to earn a K.C.B

The General got 'is decorations thick
   (The men that backed 'is lies could not complain),
The Staff 'ad D.S.O.'s till we was sick,
   An' the soldier—'ad the work to do again!
For 'e might 'ave known the District was an 'otbed,
   Instead of 'andin' over, upside-down,
To a man 'oo 'ad to fight 'alf a year to put it right,
   While the General went an' slandered 'im in town!

An' it all went into the laundry,
But it never came out in the wash.
We were sugared about by the old men
(Panicky, perishin' old men)
That 'amper an' 'inder an' scold men
For fear o' Stellenbosh!

*The more notoriously incompetent commanders used to be sent to the town of Stellenbosch, which name presently became a verb.*

## Half-Ballad of Waterval

### Non-commissioned Officers in Charge of Prisoners

When by the labour of my 'ands
   I've 'elped to pack a transport tight
With prisoners for foreign lands,
   I ain't transported with delight.
   I know it's only just an' right,
      But yet it somehow sickens me,
For I 'ave learned at Waterval*
      The meanin' of captivity.

Be'ind the pegged barb-wire strands,
   Beneath the tall electric light,
We used to walk in bare-'ead bands,
   Explainin' 'ow we lost our fight;
   An' that is what they'll do to-night
      Upon the steamer out at sea,
If I 'ave learned at Waterval
      The meanin' of captivity.

They'll never know the shame that brands—
   Black shame no livin' down makes white—
The mockin' from the sentry-stands,
   The women's laugh, the gaoler's spite.
   We are too bloomin'-much polite,
      But that is 'ow I'd 'ave us be . . .
Since I 'ave learned at Waterval
      The meanin' of captivity.

They'll get those draggin' days all right,
   Spent as a foreigner commands,
An' 'orrors of the locked-up night,
   With 'Ell's own thinkin' on their 'ands.

I'd give the gold o' twenty Rands
    (If it was mine) to set 'em free
For I 'ave learned at Waterval
    The meanin' of captivity!

*Where the majority of English prisoners were kept by the Boers.

Piet

## Regular of the Line

I do not love my Empire's foes,
    Nor call 'em angels; still,
What is the sense of 'atin' those
    'Oom you are paid to kill?
So, barrin' all that foreign lot
    Which only joined for spite,
Myself, I'd just as soon as not
    Respect the man I fight.
        Ah there, Piet!—'is trousies to 'is knees,
        'Is coat-tails lyin' level in the bullet-sprinkled breeze;
        'E does not lose 'is rifle an' 'e does not lose 'is seat,
        I've known a lot o' people ride a dam' sight worse than Piet.

I've 'eard 'im cryin' from the ground
    Like Abel's blood of old,
An' skirmished out to look, an' found
    The beggar nearly cold.
I've waited on till 'e was dead
    (Which couldn't 'elp 'im much),
But many grateful things 'e 's said
    To me for doin' such.
        Ah there, Piet! whose time 'as come to die,
        'Is carcase past rebellion, but 'is eyes inquirin' why.
        Though dressed in stolen uniform with badge o' rank complete,
        I've known a lot o' fellers go a dam' sight worse than Piet.

An' when there was n't aught to do
    But camp and cattle-guards,
I've fought with 'im the 'ole day through
    At fifteen 'undred yards;
Long afternoons o' lyin' still,
    An' 'earin' as you lay
The bullets swish from 'ill to 'ill
    Like scythes among the 'ay.
        Ah there, Piet!-be'ind 'is stony kop.

With 'is Boer bread an' biltong, an' 'is flask of awful Dop;
    'Is Mauser for amusement an' 'is pony for retreat,
    I've known a lot o' fellers shoot a dam' sight worse than Piet.

He's shoved 'is rifle 'neath my nose
    Before I'd time to think,
An' borrowed all my Sunday clo'es
    An' sent me 'ome in pink;
An' I 'ave crept (Lord, 'ow I've crept!)
    On 'ands an' knees I've gone,
And spoored and floored and caught and kept
    An' sent him to Ceylon!
        Ah there, Piet!—you've sold me many a pup,
        When week on week alternate it was you an' me "'ands up! "
        But though I never made you walk man-naked in the 'eat,
        I've known a lot of fellows stalk a dam' sight worse than Piet.

From Plewman's to Marabastad,
    From Ookiep to De Aar,
Me an' my trusty friend 'ave 'ad,
    As you might say, a war;
But seein' what both parties done
    Before 'e owned defeat,
I ain't more proud of 'avin' won,
    Than I am pleased with Piet.
        Ah there, Piet!—picked up be'ind the drive!
        The wonder wasn't 'ow 'e fought, but 'ow 'e kep' alive,
        With nothin' in 'is belly, on 'is back, or to 'is feet—
        I've known a lot o' men behave a dam' sight worse than Piet.

No more I'll 'ear 'is rifle crack
    Along the block'ouse fence—
The beggar's on the peaceful tack,
    Regardless of expense;
For countin' what 'e eats an' draws,
    An' gifts an' loans as well,
'E's gettin' 'alf the Earth, because
    'E didn't give us 'Ell!
        Ah there, Piet! with your brand-new English plough,
        Your gratis tents an' cattle, an' your most ungrateful frow,
        You've made the British taxpayer rebuild your country seat—
        I've known some pet battalions charge a dam' sight less than Piet.


"Wilful-Missing"

**Deserters of the Boer War**

There is a world outside the one you know,
    To which for curiousness 'Ell can't compare—
It is the place where "wilful-missings" go,
    As we can testify—for we are there.

You may 'ave read a bullet laid us low,
    That we was gathered in "with reverent care"
And buried proper. But it was not so,
    As we can testify,for we are there!

They can't be certain—faces alter so
    After the old aasvogel's 'ad 'is share.
The uniform 's the mark by which they go—
    And—ain't it odd?—the one we best can spare.

We might 'ave seen our chance to cut the show—
    Name, number, record, an' begin elsewhere
Leavin' some not too late-lamented foe
    One funeral—private—British—for 'is share.

We may 'ave took it yonder in the Low
    Bush-veldt that sends men stragglin' unaware
Among the Kaffirs, till their columns go,
    An' they are left past call or count or care.

We might 'ave been your lovers long ago,
    'Usbands or children—comfort or despair.
Our death (an' burial) settles all we owe,
    An' why we done it is our own affair.

Marry again, and we will not say no,
    Nor come to barstardise the kids you bear.
Wait on in 'ope—you've all your life below
    Before you'll ever 'ear us on the stair.

There is no need to give our reasons, though
    Gawd knows we all 'ad reasons which were fair;
But other people might not judge 'em so—
    And now it doesn't matter what they were.

What man can weigh or size another's woe?
    There are some things too bitter 'ard to bear.
Suffice it we 'ave finished—Domino!
    As we can testify, for we are there,
In the side-world where "wilful-missings" go.

## Royal Artillery

There is a word you often see, pronounce it as you may
"You bike," "you bykwee," "ubbikwe "— alludin' to R.A.
It serves 'Orse, Field, an' Garrison as motto for a crest,
An' when you've found out all it means I'll tell you 'alf the rest.

Ubique means the long-range Krupp be'ind the low-range 'ill—
Ubique means you'll pick it up an', while you do, stand still.
Ubique means you've caught the flash an' timed it by the sound.
Ubique means five gunners' 'ash before you've loosed a round.

Ubique means Blue Fuse an' make the 'ole to sink the trail.
Ubique means stand up an' take the Mauser's 'alf-mile 'ail.
Ubique means the crazy team not God nor man can 'old.
Ubique means that 'orse's scream which turns your innards cold!

Ubique means "Bank, 'Olborn, Bank—a penny all the way—
The soothin', jingle-bump-an'-clank from day to peaceful day.
Ubique means "They've caught De Wet, an' now we sha'n t be long."
Ubique means "I much regret, the beggar's goin' strong!"

Ubique means the tearin' drift where, breech-blocks jammed with mud,
The khaki muzzles duck an' lift across the khaki flood.
Ubique means the dancing plain that changes rocks to Boers.
Ubique means the mirage again an' shellin' all outdoors.

Ubique means "Entrain at once for Grootdefeatfontein"!
Ubique means "Off-load your guns"— at midnight in the rain!
Ubique means "More mounted men. Return all guns to store."
Ubique means the R. A. M. R. Infantillery Corps!

Ubique means that warnin' grunt the perished linesman knows,
When o'er 'is strung an' sufferin' front the shrapnel sprays 'is foes;
An' as their firin' dies away the 'usky whisper runs
From lips that 'ave n't drunk all day: "The Guns! Thank Gawd, the Guns!"

Extreme, depressed, point-blank or short, end-first or any'ow,
From Colesberg Kop to Quagga's Poort—from Ninety-Nine till now—
By what I've 'eard the others tell an' I in spots 'ave seen,
There's nothin' this side 'Eaven or 'Ell Ubique does n't mean!

## All Arms

Peace is declared, an' I return
   To 'Ackneystadt, but not the same;
Things 'ave transpired which made me learn
   The size and meanin' of the game.
I did no more than others did,
   I don't know where the change began.
I started as a average kid,
   I finished as a thinkin' man.

If England was what England seems,
   An' not the England of our dreams,
But only putty, brass, an' paint,
   'Ow quick we'd drop 'er! But she ain't!

Before my gappin' mouth could speak
   I 'eard it in my comrade's tone;
I saw it on my neighbour's cheek
   Before I felt it flush my own.
An' last it come to me—not pride,
   Nor yet conceit, but on the 'ole
(If such a term may be applied),
   The makin's of a bloomin' soul.

Rivers at night that cluck an' jeer,
   Plains which the moonshine turns to sea,
Mountains which never let you near,
   An' stars to all eternity;
An' the quick-breathin' dark that fills
   The 'ollows of the wilderness,
When the wind worries through the 'ills—
   These may 'ave taught me more or less.

Towns without people, ten times took,
   An' ten times left an' burned at last;
An' starvin' dogs that come to look
   For owners when a column passed;
An' quiet, 'omesick talks between
   Men, met by night, you never knew
Until—'is face—by shellfire seen—
   Once—an' struck off. They taught me too

The day's lay-out—the mornin' sun
   Beneath your 'at-brim as you sight;
The dinner-'ush from noon till one,
   An' the full roar that lasts till night;

An' the pore dead that look so old
  An' was so young an hour ago,
An' legs tied down before they're cold—
  These are the things which make you know.

Also Time runnin' into years—
  A thousand Places left be'ind—
An' Men from both two 'emispheres
  Discussin' things of every kind;
So much more near than I 'ad known,
  So much more great than I 'ad guessed—
An' me, like all the rest, alone—
  But reachin' out to all the rest!

So 'ath it come to me-not pride,
  Nor yet conceit, but on the 'ole
(If such a term may be applied),
  The makin's of a bloomin' soul.
But now, discharged, I fall away
  To do with little things again . . . .
Gawd, 'oo knows all I cannot say,
  Look after me in Thamesfontein!

If England was what England seems,
  An' not the England of our dreams,
But only putty, brass, an' paint,
  'Ow quick we'd chuck 'er! But she ain't!


Recessional

**A Victorian Ode**

God of our fathers, known of old,
  Lord of our far-flung battle line,
Beneath whose awful hand we hold
  Dominion over palm and pine—
Lord God of Hosts, be with us yet,
Lest we forget—lest we forget!

The tumult and the shouting dies;
  The Captains and the Kings depart;
Still stands Thine ancient sacrifice,
  An humble and a contrite heart.
Lord God of Hosts, be with us yet,
Lest we forget—lest we forget!

Far-called our navies melt away;
    On dune and headland sinks the fire;
Lo, all our pomp of yesterday
    Is one with Nineveh and Tyre!
Judge of the Nations, spare us yet,
Lest we forget—lest we forget!

If, drunk with sight of power, we loose
    Wild tongues that have not Thee in awe,
Such boastings as the Gentiles use,
    Or lesser breeds without the Law—
Lord God of Hosts, be with us yet,
Lest we forget—lest we forget!

For heathen heart that puts her trust
    In reeking tube and iron shard—
All valiant dust that builds on dust,
    And guarding calls not Thee to guard.
For frantic boast and foolish word,
Thy Mercy on Thy People, Lord!


Rudyard Kipling – A Short Biography

Born in Bombay on 30th December 1865, Joseph Rudyard Kipling wrote short stories, poems and novels, a body of work whose reputation is in constant flux as his presentations and interpretations of empire are viewed within the changing context of empirical absolution in the twentieth century. Having spent the first five years of his life in India he felt a natural affinity for the country, though his upbringing had a distinctly colonial taste flavour. He was born in the Bombay Presidency of British India to Lockwood Kipling, an English art teacher and illustrator who took a position as professor of architectural sculpture in the Jeejeebhoy School of Art and Alice MacDonald, spoken of by the a Viceroy of India that "dullness and Mrs Kipling cannot exist in the same room". Though their presence in India was principally artistic and educational, rather than political, the company they kept and the establishments in which they kept it indicate an existence very much benefitting from the British Empire. Lockwood would later go on to assume a position as curator of the Lahore Museum, while working on various illustrations for Rudyard's writing, and various decorations for the Victoria and Albert museum in London. Much of his work, then, was coloured by the empire, whether in service to or benefitting from, and it was into this distinctly British experience of India that Rudyard was born.

Lockwood and Alice had met and fallen in love at Rudyard Lake in Rudyard, Staffordshire, and their affections for the area were so great they chose to refer to the lake in naming their first-born. Alice came from a family of four sisters, all of whose marriages were significant and well-arranged; moreover, Rudyard's most famous relative was Stanley Baldwin, Conservative Prime Minister on three occasions in the 1920s and 1930s. Kipling's sense of belonging in Bombay is found in 'To the City of Bombay' in the dedication to Seven Seas, a collection of poems published in 1900, which reads:—

Mother of Cities to me,

For I was born in her gate,
Between the palms and the sea,
Where the world-end steamers wait.

His parents considered themselves Anglo-Indians, and he would later assume this classification although he did not live there long. His first five years, which he describes as days of "strong light and darkness", ended when he and his three-year-old sister Alice were removed to Southsea, Plymouth, to board with Captain Pryse Agar Holloway and his wife Mrs Sarah Holloway, a couple who cared for the children of couples born in British India. They were there for six years and Kipling would later recall their time there with horror, describing incidents of cruelty and neglect and wondering whether it was these which speeded up his literary maturity, for "it made me give attention to the lies I soon found it necessary to tell: and this, I presume, is the foundation of literary effort".

Alice's time, by contrast, was relatively comfortable, Mrs Holloway hoping that she would marry her son, though this ambition would not come to fruition. They did have relatives in England, a maternal aunt Georgiana and her husband who lived in Fulham, London, in a house at which they spent a month each Christmas and which Kipling later described as "a paradise which I verily believe saved me". Their mother returned in 1877 and removed them from their custody with the Holloways. A year later he gained admission to the United Services College at Westward Ho! in Devon, a recently established school with the intention of readying boys for military service in the British Army. His time here was fraught physically, though emotionally it proved fruitful for he began several firm friendships with other boys at the school. Moreover, he found in it inspiration for the setting of his series of schoolboy stories, Stalky and Co, begun in 1899. Meanwhile, his sister Alice had returned to Southsea and was boarding with Florence Garrard, with whom he fell in love and on whom he modeled Maisie in his first novel, The Light That Failed, published in 1891. At sixteen he was found lacking in the academic perspicacity necessary to undertake a scholarship to Oxford University, his parents meanwhile lacking the wherewithal to finance him therein. As such his father sought a job for him in Lahore, Punjab, where he was now a museum curator. The position he found for his son was as assistant editor of the Civil and Military Gazette, a small local newspaper. Kipling left for India on 20th September 1882, arriving in Bombay on 18th October. "There were yet three or four days" rail to Lahore, where my people lived. After these, my English years fell away, nor ever, I think, came back in full strength".

The Gazette appeared six days of the week, year-round save for a short break at both Christmas and Easter. Its editor Stephen Wheeler was diligent but Kipling's writing was insatiable, and he came to consider the paper his "mistress and most true love". In the summer of 1883 Kipling visited Shimla, the colonial hill-station and summer capital of British India which was then called Simla. Chosen by the British owing to its resemblance of English climate and scenery (as far as was possible in India), it became the seat of the Viceroy of India for the six months on the plains which were too hot for the British temperament, and subsequently became a "centre of power as well as pleasure". Lockwood was asked to serve in the Church there, and his family became yearly visitors while Kipling himself would take his annual leave here from 1885-88. The value of this time is evident from the regularity with which Simla appears in his writing for the Gazette, which in his journals he describes the time as

> "….pure joy—every golden hour counted. It began in heat and discomfort, by rail and road. It ended in the cool evening, with a wood fire in one's bedroom, and next morn—thirty more of them ahead!—the early cup of tea, the Mother who brought it in, and the long talks of us all together again."

In 1886, his Departmental Ditties appeared, his first collection of verse, and brought with it a change of editor; Kay Robinson, Wheeler's replacement, was in favour of Kipling's creativity and granted him more freedom in that respect, even asking him to write short stories to appear in the newspaper. The vivacity of his writing was captured in a description of him by an ex-colleague at the Gazette, saying he "never knew such a fellow for ink—he simply revelled in it, filling up his pen viciously, and then throwing the contents all over the office, so that it was almost dangerous to approach him". While in Lahore, he had thirty-nine stories published in the Gazette between November 1886 and June 1887. Most of these are compiled in Plain Tales from the Hills, his first collection of prose, which was published in January 1888 in Calcutta, shortly after his 22nd birthday. In November 1887, he transferred from the Gazette to its much larger sister newspaper, The Pioneer, based in Allahabad. The pace of his writing remained, and in 1888 he published six collections of stories, Soldiers Three, The Story of the Gadsbys, In Black and White, Under the Deodars, The Phantom Rickshaw and Wee Willie Winkie, composed of some 41 stories. In addition, his position as The Pioneer's special correspondent in the Western region of Rajputna, he wrote many sketches which were later compiled in Letters of Marque and published in From Sea to Sea and Other Sketches, Letters of Travel.

A dispute in 1889 saw him discharged from The Pioneer, though by now he had been considering his future and sold the rights to his six volumes of stories for £200 and a small royalty, while the Plain Tales fetched £50, along with six months' salary from The Pioneer in lieu of notice. Using the money to undertake a pilgrimage to London, the literary centre of the British Empire, he left India on 9th March 1889, travelling via Rangoon, San Francisco, Hong Kong and Japan, then through the United States writing articles for The Pioneer which were also included in From Sea to Sea and Other Sketches, Letters of Travel. Arriving in England at Liverpool on October 1889, London and his literary début there beckoned.

His first task was to find a place to live, and he eventually settled on quarters in Villiers Street, Strand. The next two years saw several stories accepted by various magazine editors, the publication of the novel The Light That Failed, a nervous breakdown, the collaboration with Wolcott Balestier on the novel (uncharacterstically misspelt) The Naulhaka, and in 1891, following his doctors' advice, he embarked on a further sea voyage, travelling to South Africa, Australia, New Zealand and also returning to India. His plans to spend Christmas with his family were cut short on the news of Balestier's sudden death from typhoid fever, prompting an immediate return to London. Before he left, he had proposed to Balestier's sister Caroline Starr Balestier, with whom he had been having a hushed romance for just over a year. Back in London, Life's Handicap was published in 1891, a collection of short stories whose subject was the British in India, and British India. On 18th January 1892 aged 26 he married Caroline in the midst of an epidemic of influenza. Caroline was given away by Henry James, the famous and celebrated American author.

Honeymooning in Japan, they travelled via Vermont, America, to visit the Balestier estate, and upon arrival in Yokahama they found that their bank, The New Oriental Banking Corporation, had failed, though this loss did not deter them and they returned to Vermont, Caroline now pregnant with their first child. Renting a cottage on a farm for $10 per month, they lived a spartan existence and were "extraordinarily and self-centredly content". The named the residence Bliss Cottage, and it was here that the child was born, named Josephine, "in three foot of snow on the night of 29th December 1892. Her Mother's birthday being the 31st and mine the 30th we congratulated her on her sense of the fitness of things." While here, Kipling had his first ideas for the Jungle Books. Shortly after Josephine was born the couple moved in pursuit of more space and comfort, buying ten acres overlooking the Connecticut River from Caroline's brother. The house they built there was inspired by the Mughul architecture he encountered in Lahore, and was named Naulakha (this time correctly spelt) in honour of Wolcott. His literary output in four years here included the Jungle Books, a collection of short stories entitled The Day's Work, the novel Captain Courageous and a plethora of poetry, of which most notably the volume The Seven Seas and his Barrack-Room Ballads. Meanwhile, he enjoyed correspondence with the many children who wrote to him about the Jungle Books.

In between this writing, Kipling took regular visitors. Most notably Arthur Conan Doyle came, bringing golf clubs and staying for two days to give Kipling an extended golf lesson. Kipling enjoyed the game so much that he continued to play, even in winter with special red balls, though he found that the ice would lead to drives travelling two miles as they slid "down the long slope to the Connecticut River". Elsie, the couple's second daughter, was born in February 1896, and by this time it is thought that their marriage had lost its original spark of spontaneity and descended into routine, though they remained loyal to one another. By now, failed arbitration between the United States and England over a border dispute involving British Guiana incited Anglo-American tensions which, in May 1896, resulted in a confrontation between Kipling and Caroline's brother, resulting in his arrest and, in the hearing which followed, the destruction of Kipling's private life, leaving him exhausted and miserable and leading to their return to England.

They had settled Torquay, Devon, by September 1896, and he remained socially present and literarily productive. The success of his writing had brought him fame, and he had responded with a sense of duty to include in his writing elements of political persuasion, most notably in his two poems Recessional and The White Man's Burden, which caused controversy when they were published in 1897 and 1899 respectively. Many considered them anthemic to the empire, propaganda for the imperial mindset so prevalent in the Victoria era. Their first son, John, was born in August 1887. Another journey to South Africa began a tradition of wintering there, which continued until 1908. His reputation as Poet of the Empire saw him well-received by politicians in the Cape Colony, and he started the newspaper The Friend for Lord Roberts and the British troops in Bloemfontein. Back in England, they moved to Rottingdean, East Sussex, in 1897, and in 1902 he bought Bateman's, a house built in 1630, which was his home from until his death in 1936. Kim was published in 1902, after which he collected material for Just So Stories for Little Children, published a year later. Both he and Josephine developed pneumonia while visiting the United States, from which she later died.

This decade proved his most successful, being awarded the Nobel Prize for Literature in 1907, the prize citation reading "in consideration of the power of observation, originality of imagination, virility of ideas and remarkable talent for narration which characterise the creations of this world-famous author". He was the first English-language recipient. At the award ceremony in Switzerland, Carl David af Wirsén praised Kipling and the English literary tradition:

> The Swedish Academy, in awarding the Nobel Prize in Literature this year to Rudyard Kipling, desires to pay a tribute to the literature of England, so rich in manifold glories, and to the greatest genius in the realm of narrative that that country has produced in our times.

Following this achievement, Kipling published Rewards and Fairies, which contained If, voted Britain's favourite poem in a BBC opinion poll in 1995. He turned down several recommendations for knighthood and was considered for Poet Laureate, though this position was never offered to him.

The sense of perseverance, honour and stoicism in If prevailed in many of his opinions, including that on the First World War. Writing in The New Army in Training in 1915, he scorned those who refused conscription, considering

> ....what will be the position in years to come of the young man who has deliberately elected to outcaste himself from this all-embracing brotherhood? What of his family, and, above all, what of his descendants, when the books have been closed and the last balance struck of sacrifice and sorrow in every hamlet, village, parish, suburb, city, shire, district, province, and Dominion throughout the Empire?

This attitude saw him encourage his son, John, to go to war, and he was promptly killed at the Battle of Loos in September 1915, aged 18. Last seen during the battle stumbling blindly through the mud, screaming in agony after an exploding shell had ripped his face apart, Kipling would write—

"If any question why we died
Tell them, because our fathers lied"

—perhaps betraying the guilt he felt at encouraging his son to go to war and finding him a position in the Irish Guards through his friendship with commander-in-chief Lord Roberts, for whom he had established The Friend in Bloemfontein. His death inspired much of Kipling's successive writing, notably My Boy Jack and a two-volume history of the Irish Guards, considered one of the finest examples of regimental history. Ironically, though his writing and his political position had arguably cost John his life, after the war he became friends with a French soldier whose copy of Kim, kept in his breast pocket, had stopped a bullet and saved his life. For a while the book and the soldier's Croix de Guerre were with Kipling, presented as tokens of gratitude, and they remained in contact, though when Kipling learned of the soldier's child he insisted on returning both book and medal.

He kept writing until 1930, though at a considerably slower pace, and to less success. His death, already once incorrectly announced early by a magazine in a premature obituary (and to which he responded "I've just read that I am dead. Don't forget to delete me from your list of subscribers") came on 18th January 1936, at the age of 70, from a perforated duodenal ulcer. His coffin was carried by, among others, his cousin the Prime Minister Stanley Baldwin, and his marble casket covered by a Union flag. He was cremated at Golders Green Crematorium in Northwest London and his ashes are buried at Poets' Corner in Westminster Abbey, alongside the graves of both Charles Dickens and Thomas Hardy.

In conjunction with various earthly memorials which commemorate him, alongside his extensive writing, he has a crater on Mercury named after him. The question of memorial and monument is much-addressed in English Literature and, as various great authors and poets have agreed before Kipling's time, his memory lives on more vivaciously set in his words, far longer and better represented than it could set in stone.


Rudyard Kipling - A Concise Bibliography

Books
The City of Dreadful Night (1885, short story)
Plain Tales from the Hills (1888)

Soldiers Three (1888)

The Story of the Gadsbys (1888)

In Black and White (1888)

Under the Deodars (1888)

The Phantom 'Rickshaw and other Eerie Tales (1888)

Wee Willie Winkie and Other Child Stories (1888)

Life's Handicap (1891)

The Light that Failed (1891) (novel)

American Notes (1891) (non-fiction)

The Naulahka: A Story of West and East (1892) (with Wolcott Balestie)

Many Inventions (1893)

The Jungle Book (1894)

Mowgli's Brothers (short story)

Kaa's Hunting (short story)

Tiger! Tiger! (short story)

The White Seal (short story)

Rikki-Tikki-Tavi (short story)

Toomai of the Elephants (short story)

Her Majesty's Servants (originally titled Servants of the Queen) (short story)

The Second Jungle Book (1895)

How Fear Came (short story)

The Miracle of Purun Bhagat (short story)

Letting in the Jungle (short story)

The Undertakers (short story)

The King's Ankus (short story)

Quiquern (short story)

Red Dog" (short story)

The Spring Running (short story)

Captains Courageous (1896) (novel)

The Day's Work (1898)

A Fleet in Being (1898)

Stalky & Co. (1899)

From Sea to Sea and Other Sketches, Letters of Travel (1899) (non-fiction)

Kim (1901) (novel)

Just So Stories for Little Children (1902)

Traffics and Discoveries (1904) (24 collected short stories)

With the Night Mail (1905) A Story of 2000 A.D

Puck of Pook's Hill (1906)

The Brushwood Boy (1907)

Actions and Reactions (1909)

A Song of the English (1909) (with W. Heath Robinson illustrator)

Rewards and Fairies (1910)

A History of England (1911) (non-fiction with Charles Robert Leslie Fletcher)

Songs from Books (1912)

As Easy as A.B.C. (1912) (Science-fiction short story)

The Fringes of the Fleet (1915) (non-fiction)

Sea Warfare (1916) (non-fiction)

A Diversity of Creatures (1917)

Land and Sea Tales for Scouts and Guides (1923)
The Irish Guards in the Great War (1923) (non-fiction)
Debits and Credits (1926)
A Book of Words (1928) (non-fiction)
Thy Servant a Dog (1930)
Limits and Renewals (1932)
Tales of India: the Windermere Series (1935)
Something of Myself (1937) (autobiography)
The Elephant's Child (fiction)


## Autobiographies and Speeches
A Book of Words (1928)
Something of Myself (1937)


## Short Story Collections
Quartette (1885) – with his father, mother, and sister
Plain Tales from the Hills (1888)
Soldiers Three, The Story of the Gadsbys, In Black and White (1888)
The Phantom 'Rickshaw and other Eerie Tales (1888)
Under the Deodars (1888)
Wee Willie Winkie and Other Child Stories (1888)
Life's Handicap (1891)
Many Inventions (1893)
The Jungle Book (1894)
The Second Jungle Book (1895)
The Day's Work (1898)
Life's Handicap (1899)
Stalky & Co. (1899)
Just So Stories (1902)
Traffics and Discoveries (1904)
Puck of Pook's Hill (1906)
Actions and Reactions (1909)
Abaft the Funnel (1909)
Rewards and Fairies (1910)
The Eyes of Asia (1917)
A Diversity of Creatures (1917)
Land and Sea Tales for Scouts and Guides (1923)
Debits and Credits (1926)
Thy Servant a Dog (1930)
Limits and Renewals (1932)


## Military Collections
A Fleet in Being (1898)
France at War (1915)
The New Army in Training (1915)

Sea Warfare (1916)
The War in the Mountains (1917)
The Graves of the Fallen (1919)
The Irish Guards in the Great War (1923)


## Poetry Collections
Schoolboy Lyrics (1881)
Echoes (1884) – with his sister, Alice ('Trix')
Departmental Ditties (1886)
Barrack-Room Ballads (1890)
The Seven Seas (1896)
An Almanac of Twelve Sports (1898, with illustrations by William Nicholson)
The Five Nations (1903)
Collected Verse (1907)
Songs from Books (1912)
The Years Between (1919)
Rudyard Kipling's Verse: Definitive Edition (1940)
The Muse Among the Motors (poetry)


## Travel Writing
From Sea to Sea – Letters of Travel: 1887–1889 (1899)
Letters of Travel: 1892–1913 (1920)
Souvenirs of France (1933)
Brazilian Sketches: 1927 (1940)


## Collected Works
The Outward Bound Edition (1897–1937, 36 volumes)
The Edition de Luxe (1897–1937, 38 volumes)
The Bombay Edition (1913–38, 31 volumes)
The Sussex Edition (1937–39, 35 volumes)
The Burwash Edition (1941, 28 volumes)


## Poems
Departmental Ditties and Other Verses (1886)
Barrack Room Ballads (1889, republished with additions at later times)
The Seven Seas and Further Barrack-Room Ballads (In various editions 1891–96)
The Five Nations (with some new and some reprinted and revised poems, 1903)
Twenty-two original 'Historical Poems' (1911)
Songs from Books (1912)
The Years Between (1919)


## Posthumous Collections
Rudyard Kipling's Verse: Definitive edition

A Choice of Kipling's Verse, edited by T.S. Eliot

In addition Kipling wrote and published many hundreds of poems too numerous to include here.

www.ingramcontent.com/pod-product-compliance
Lightning Source LLC
Chambersburg PA
CBHW021937040426
42448CB00008B/1120